AF380627

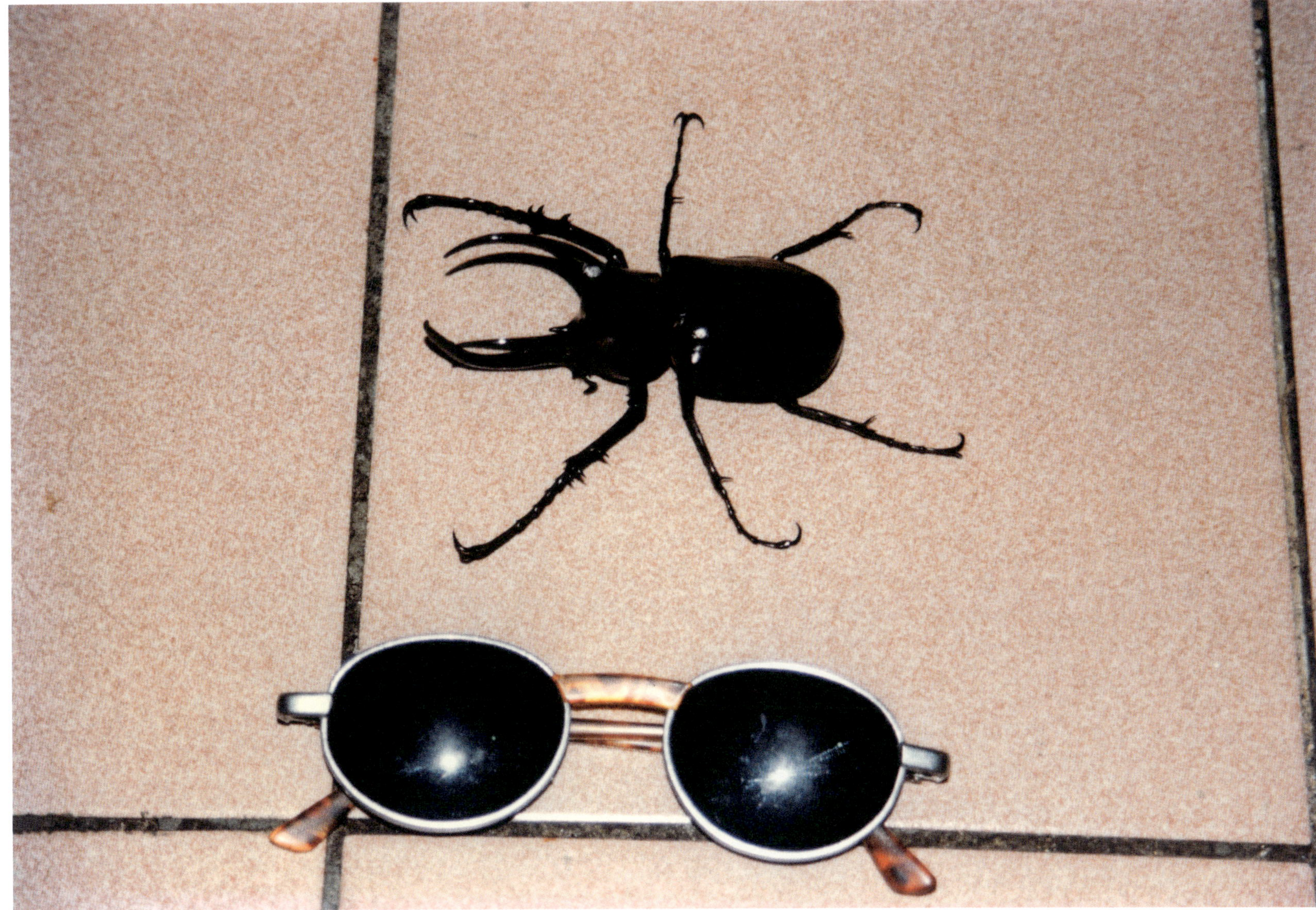

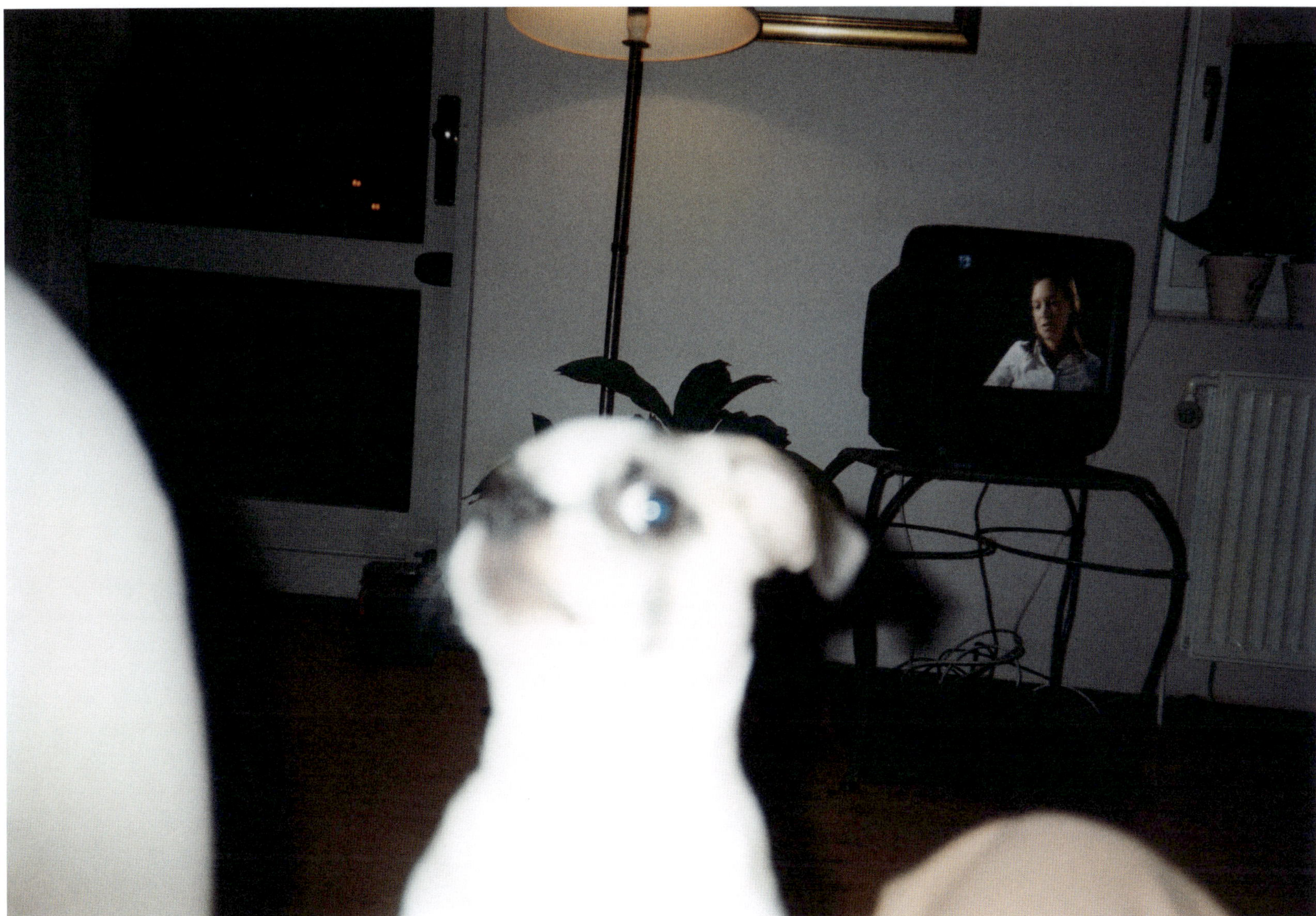

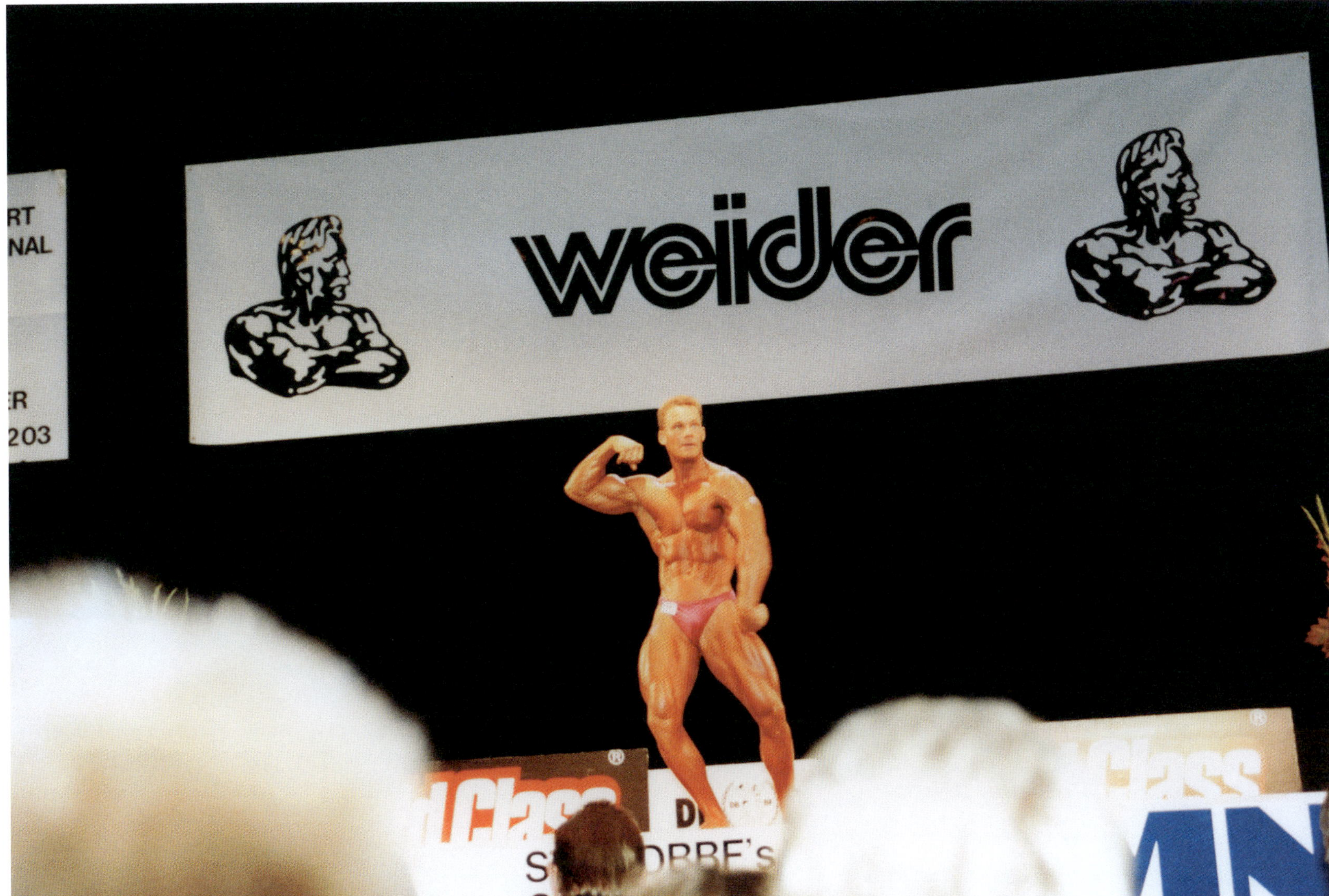

weider
203

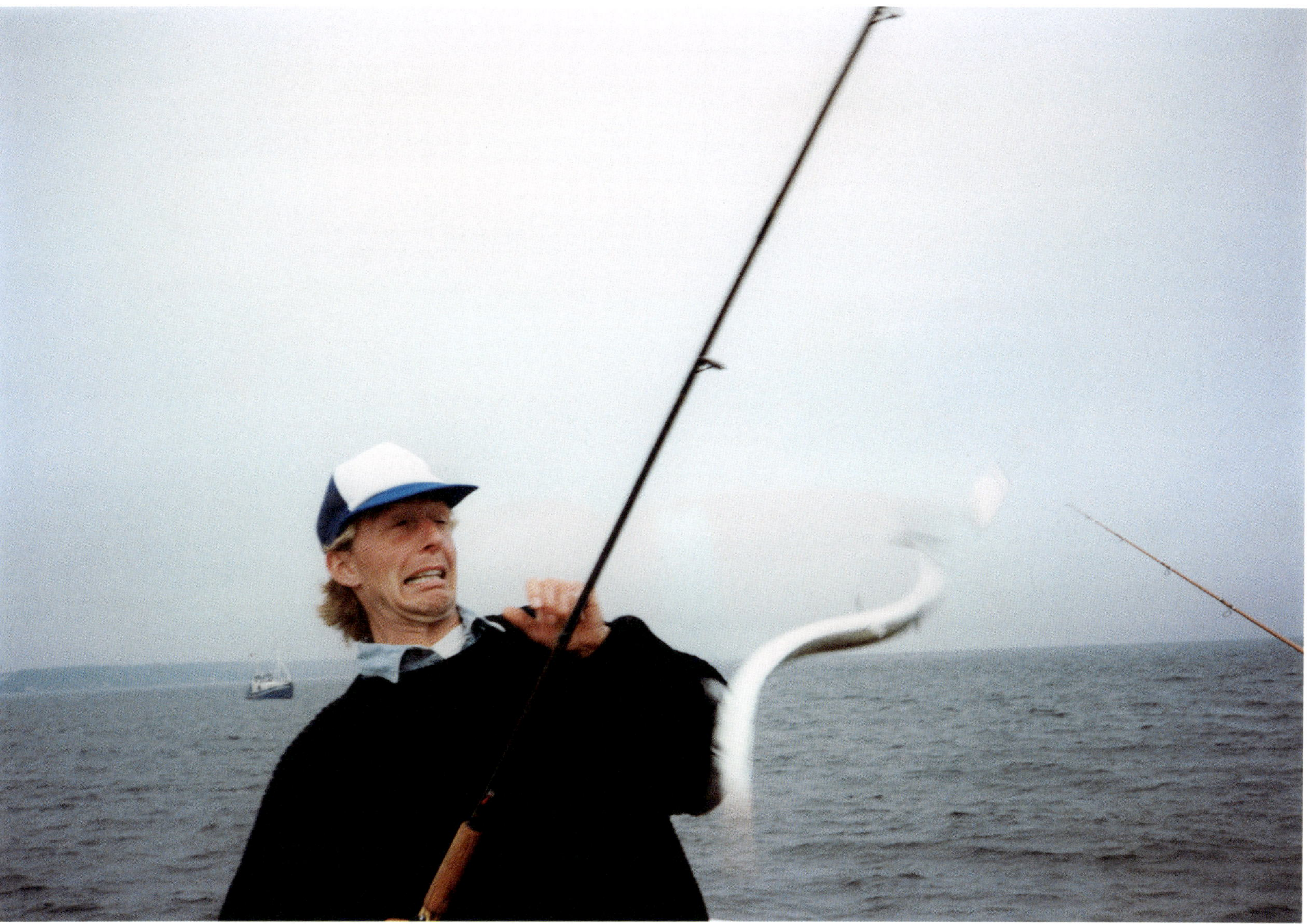

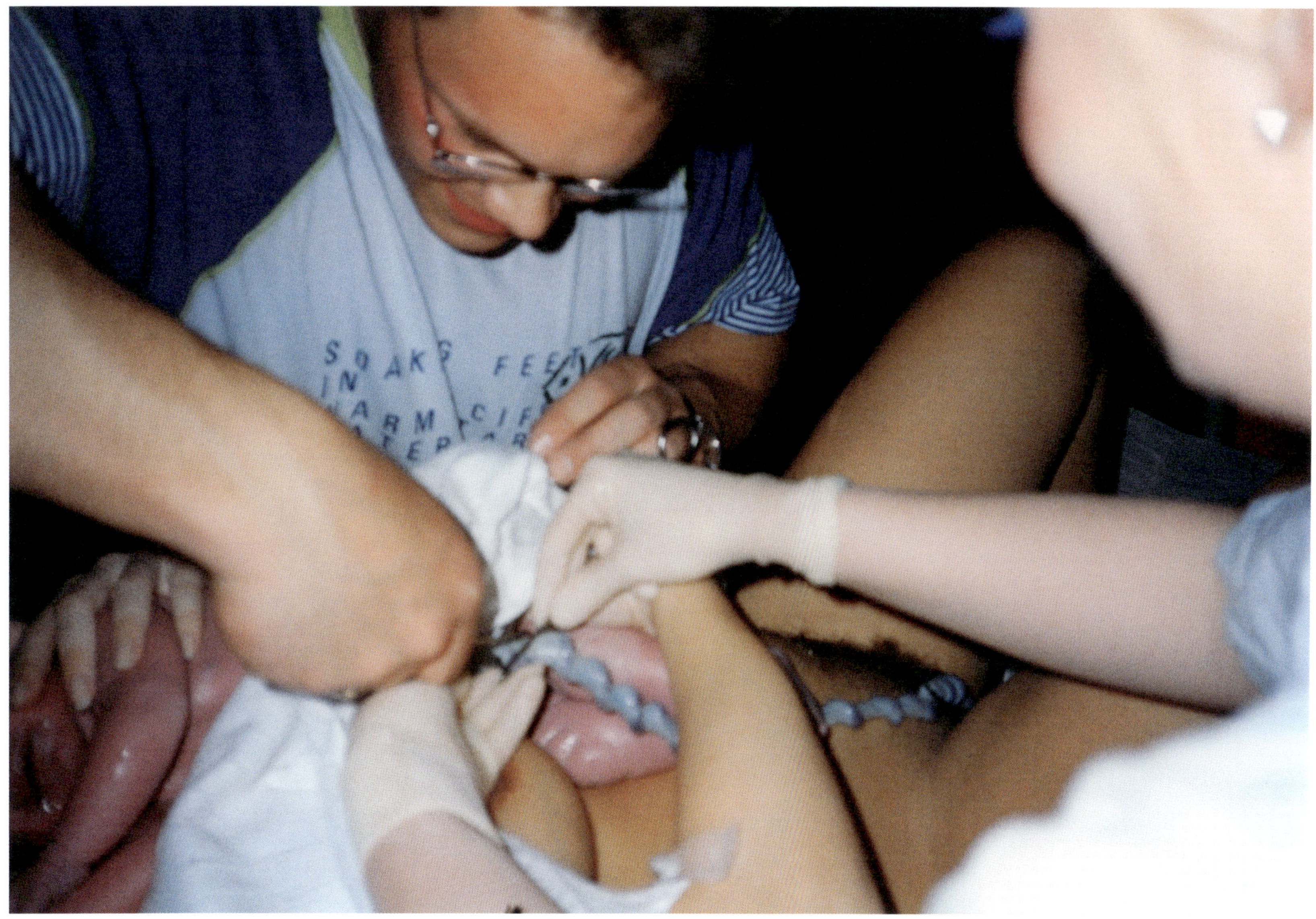

SOAK FEET
IN
WARM C...
...EP...R

Hello "Soul mate"

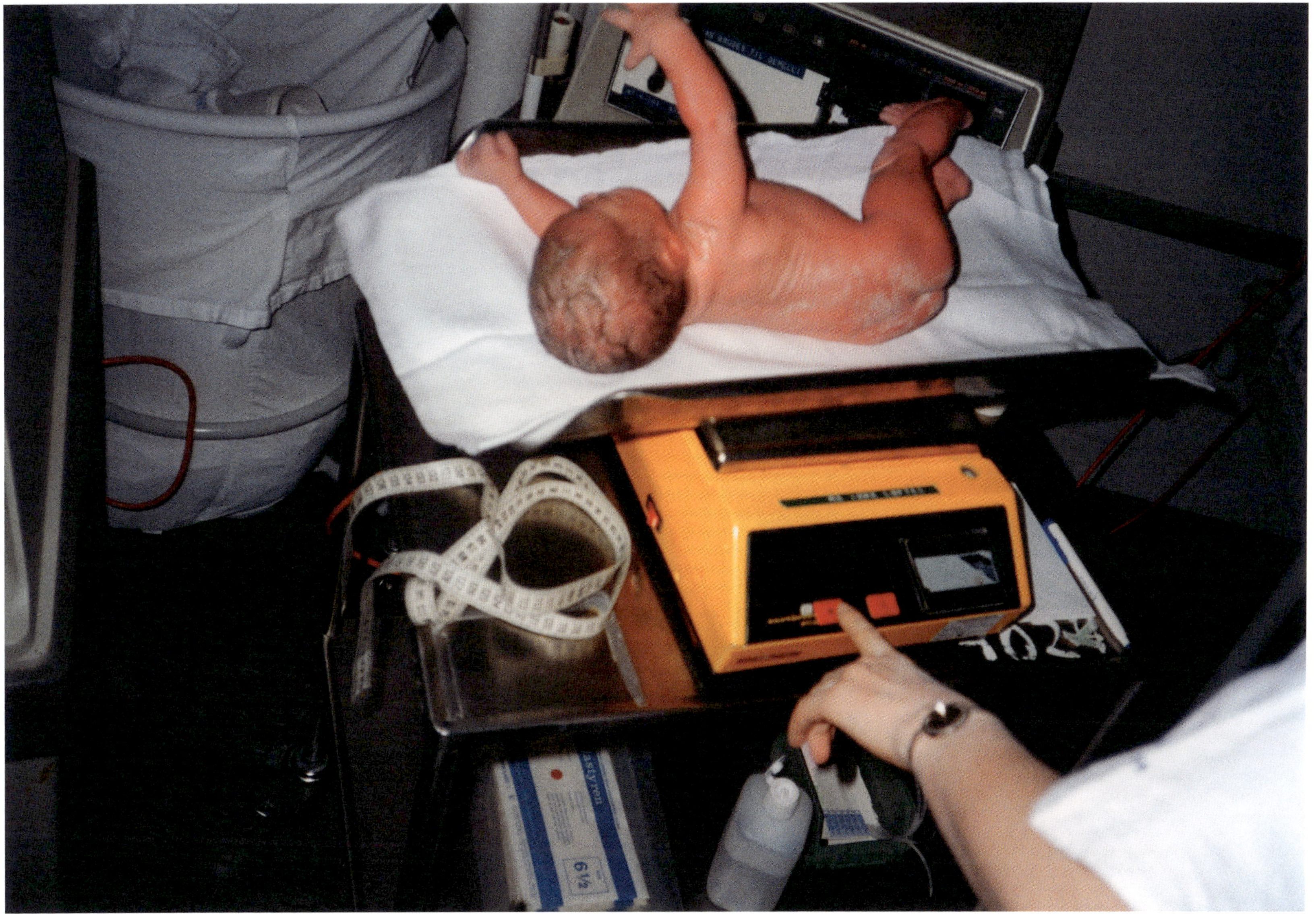

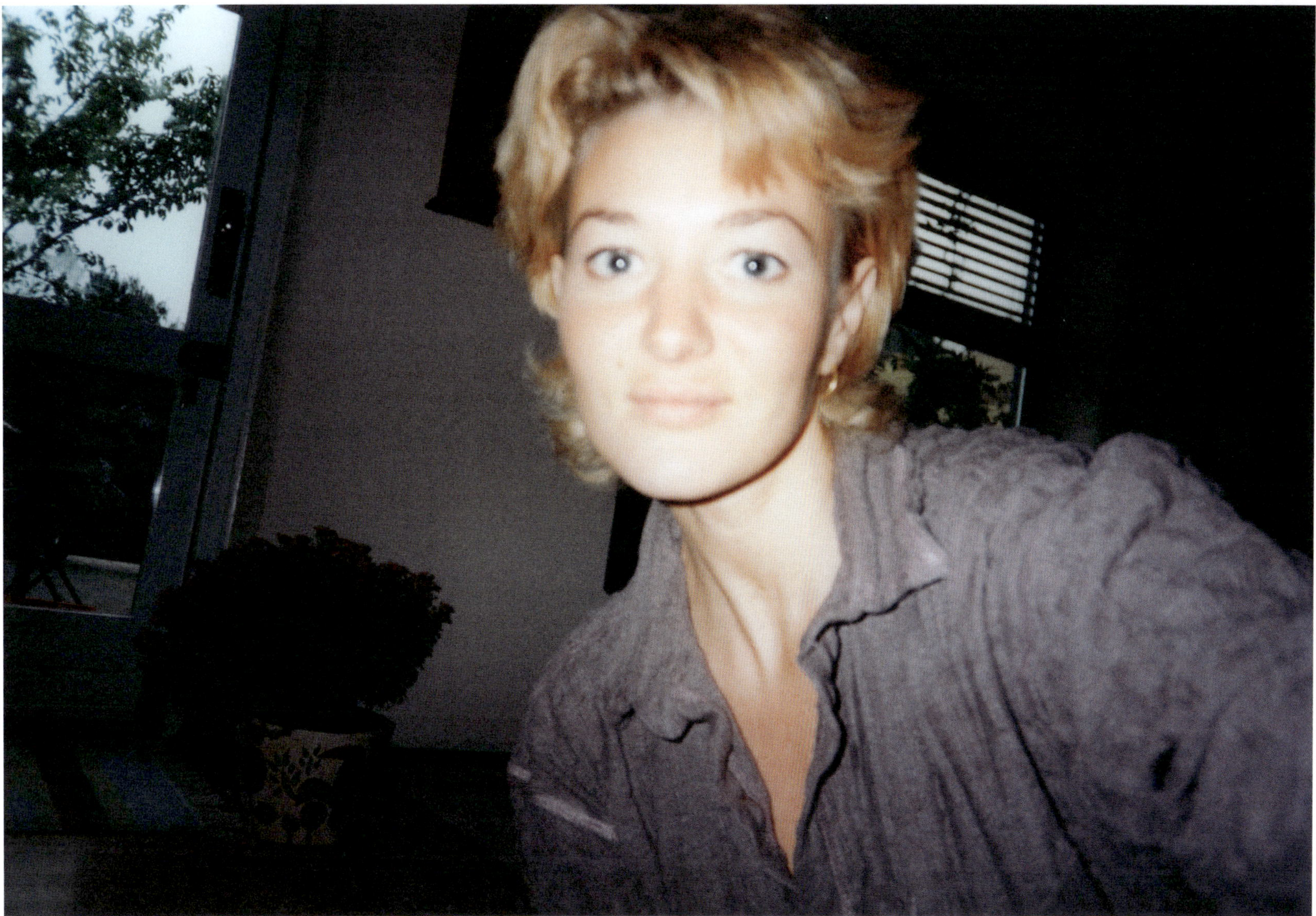

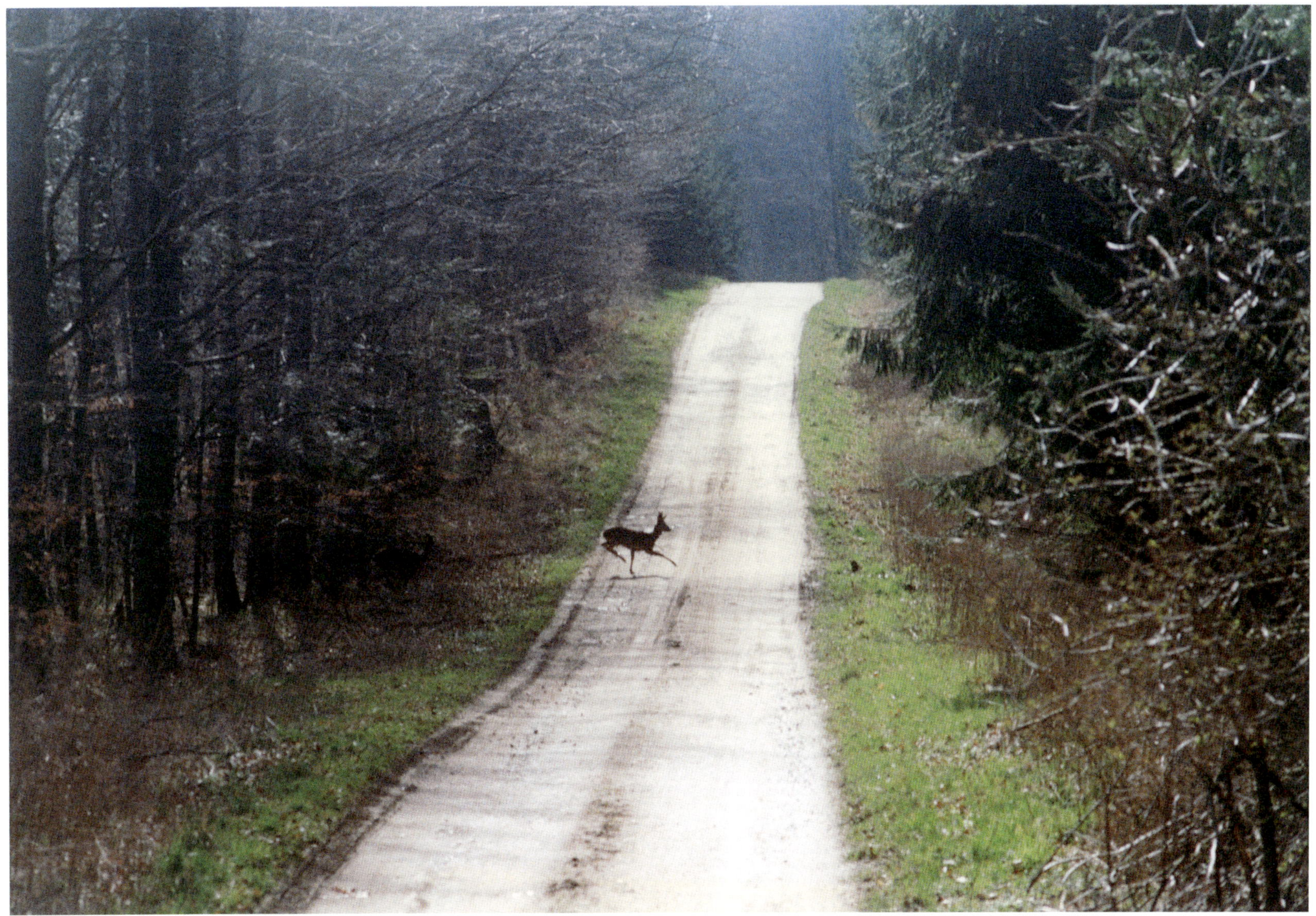

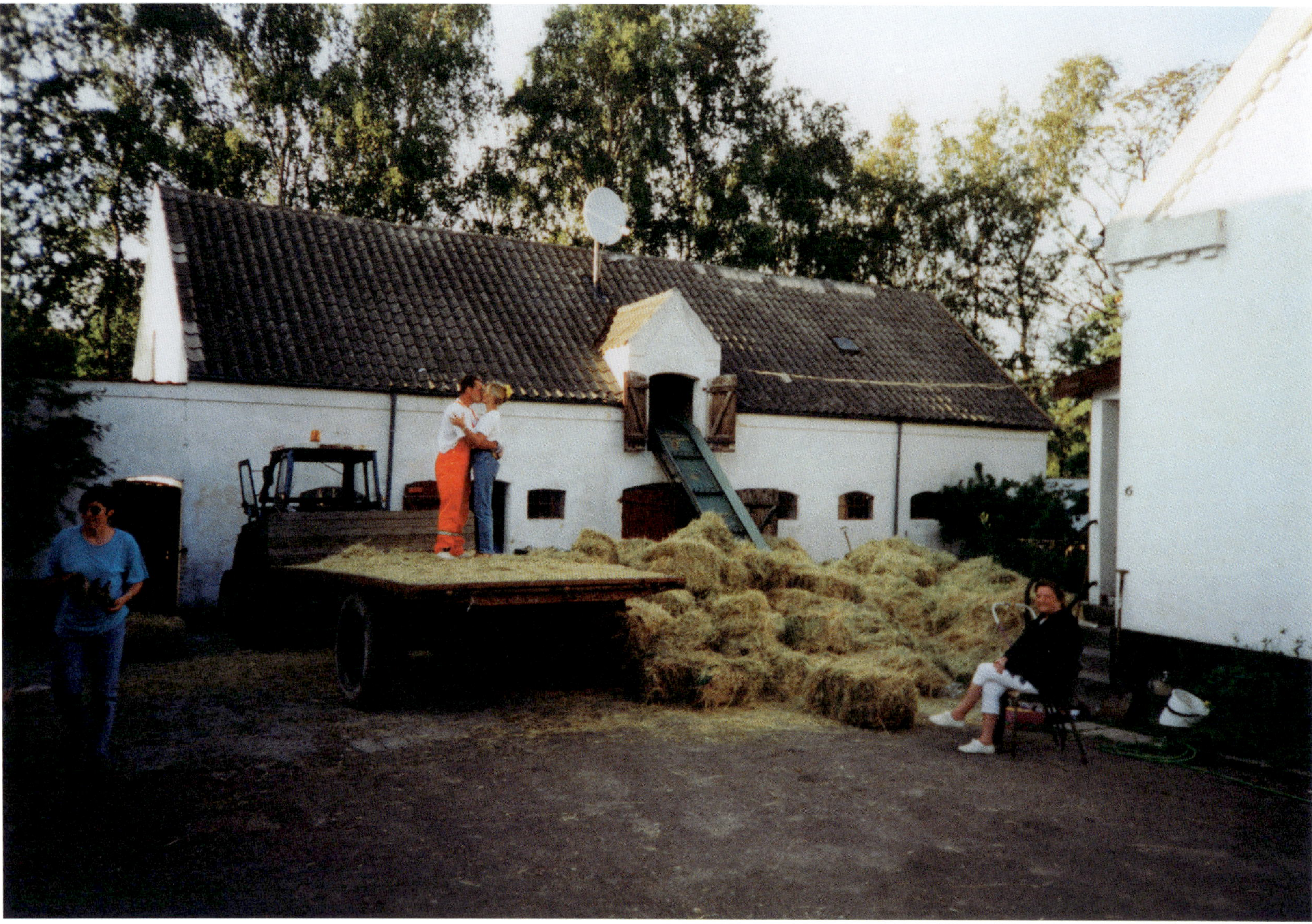

The reason why I haven't written until now is because I have been so busy.

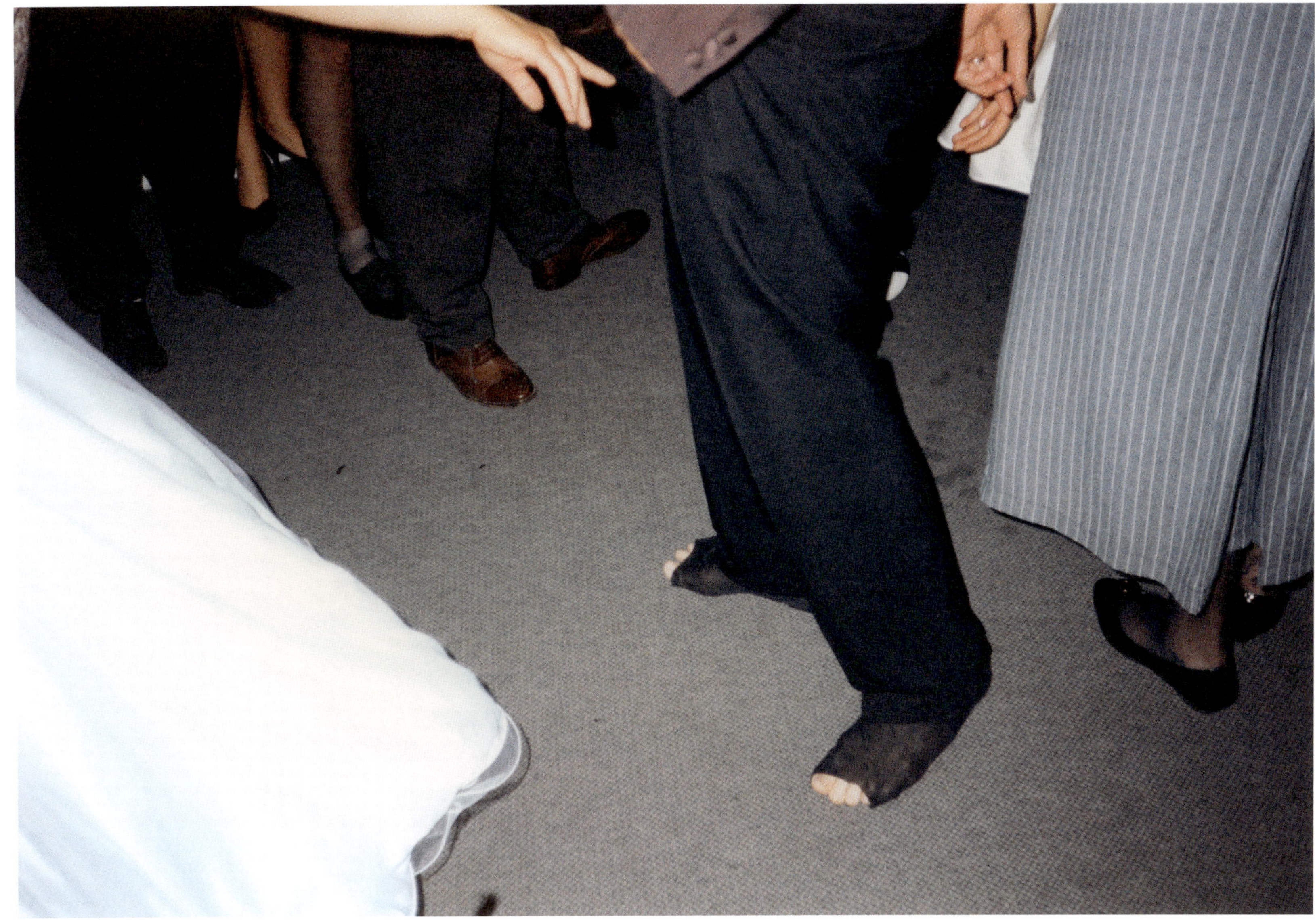

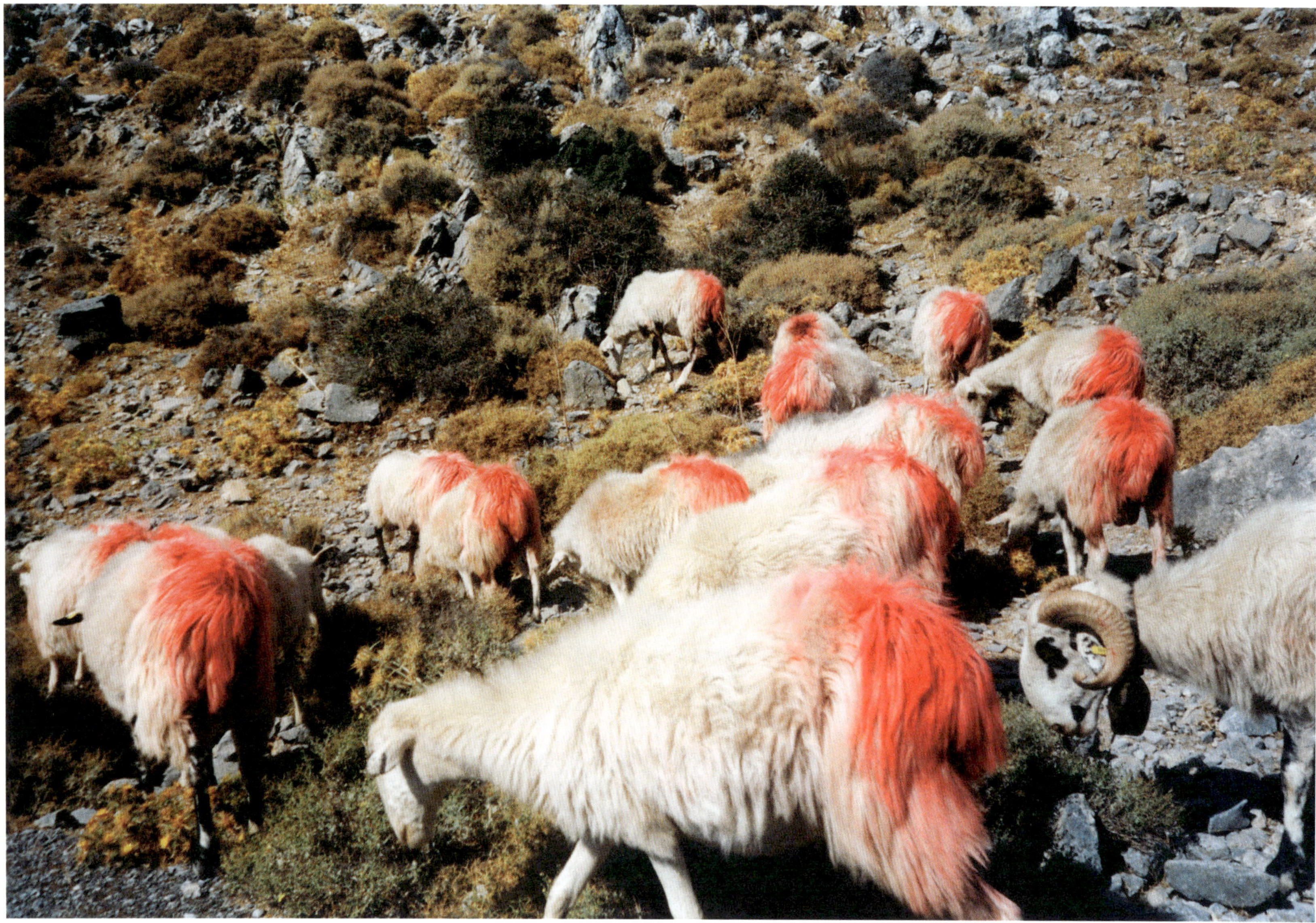

It is difficult to express how
you feel on paper.

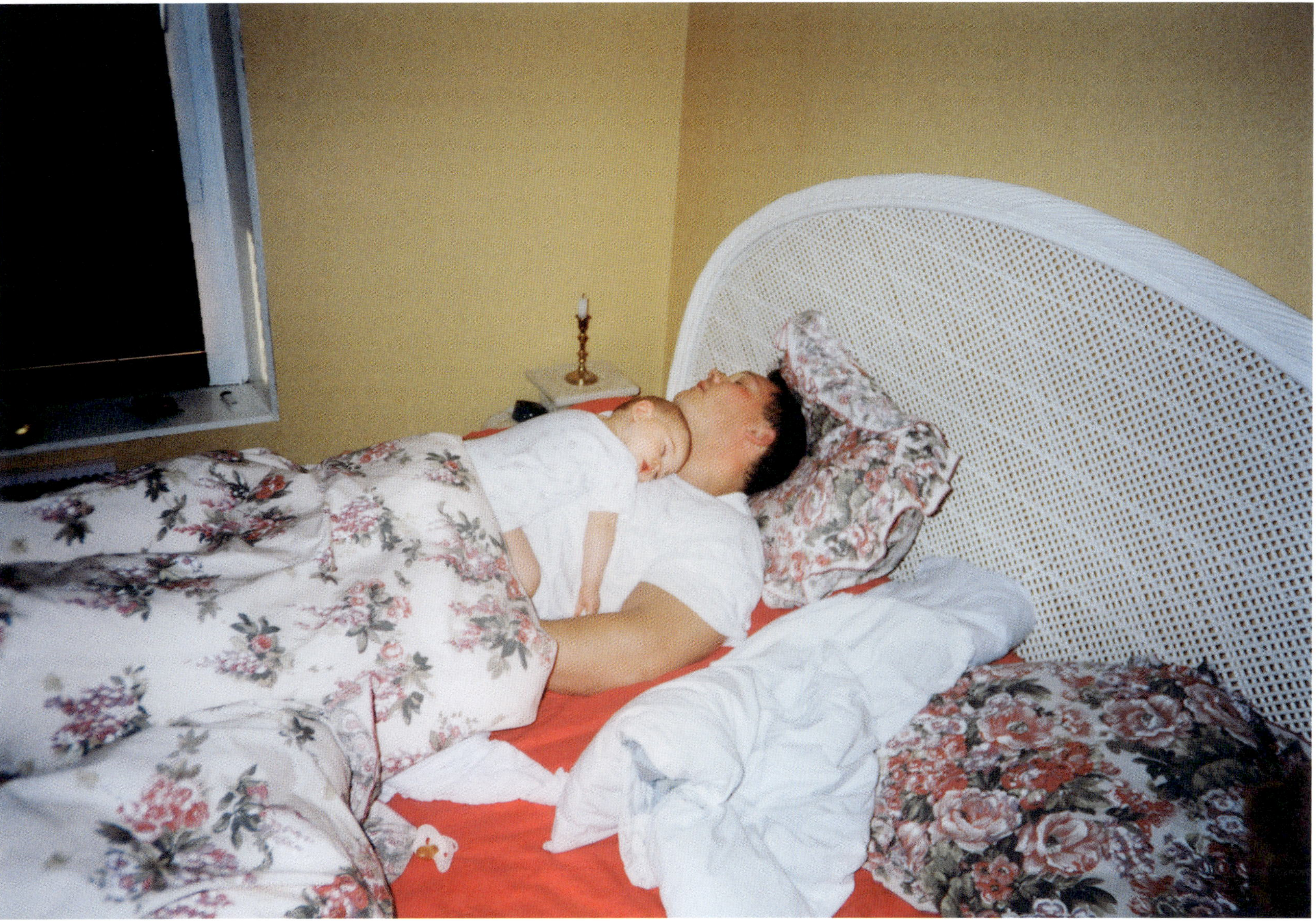

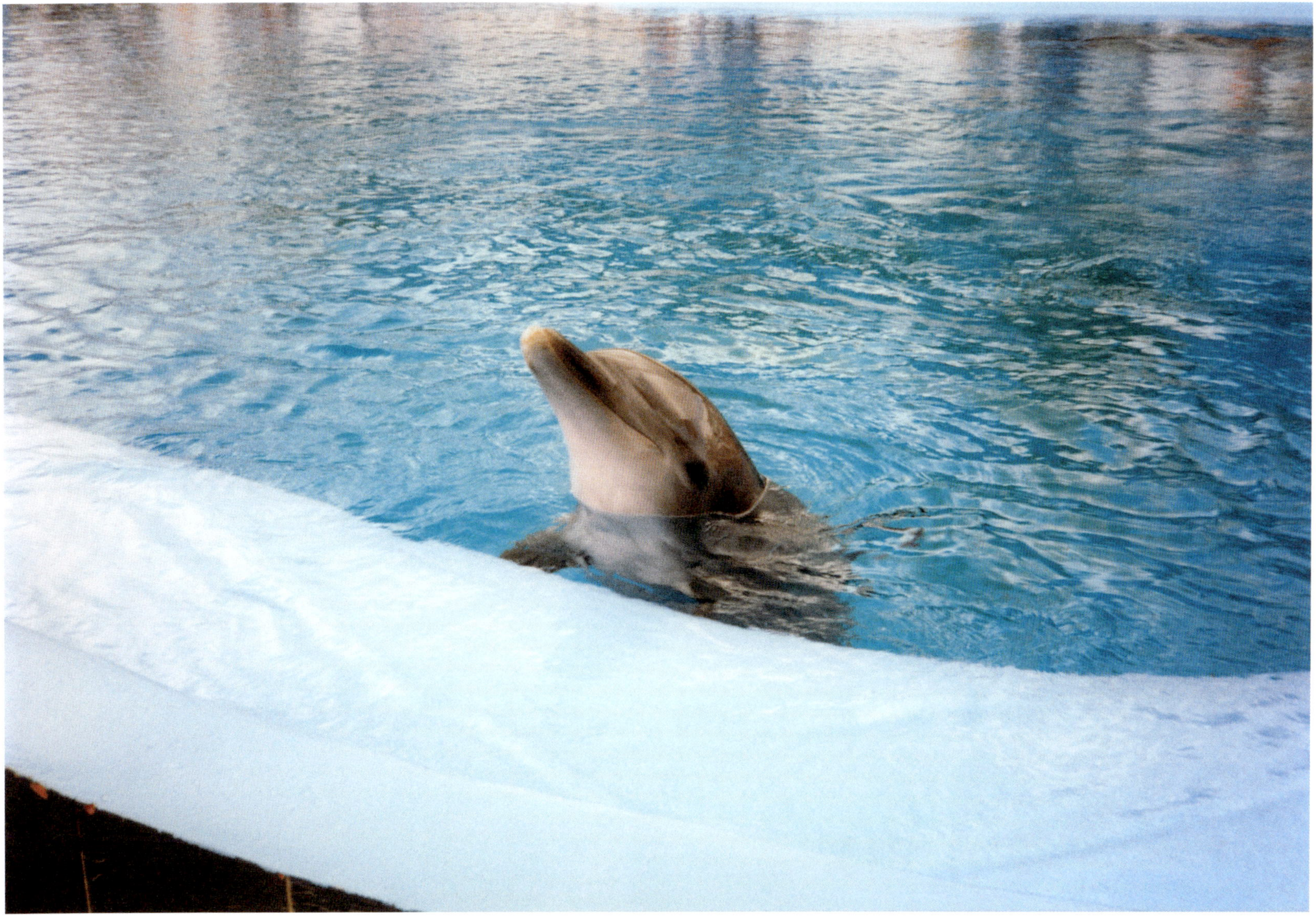

But never mind, the main thing is that being told "someone thinks and loves one" makes it much easier to endure.

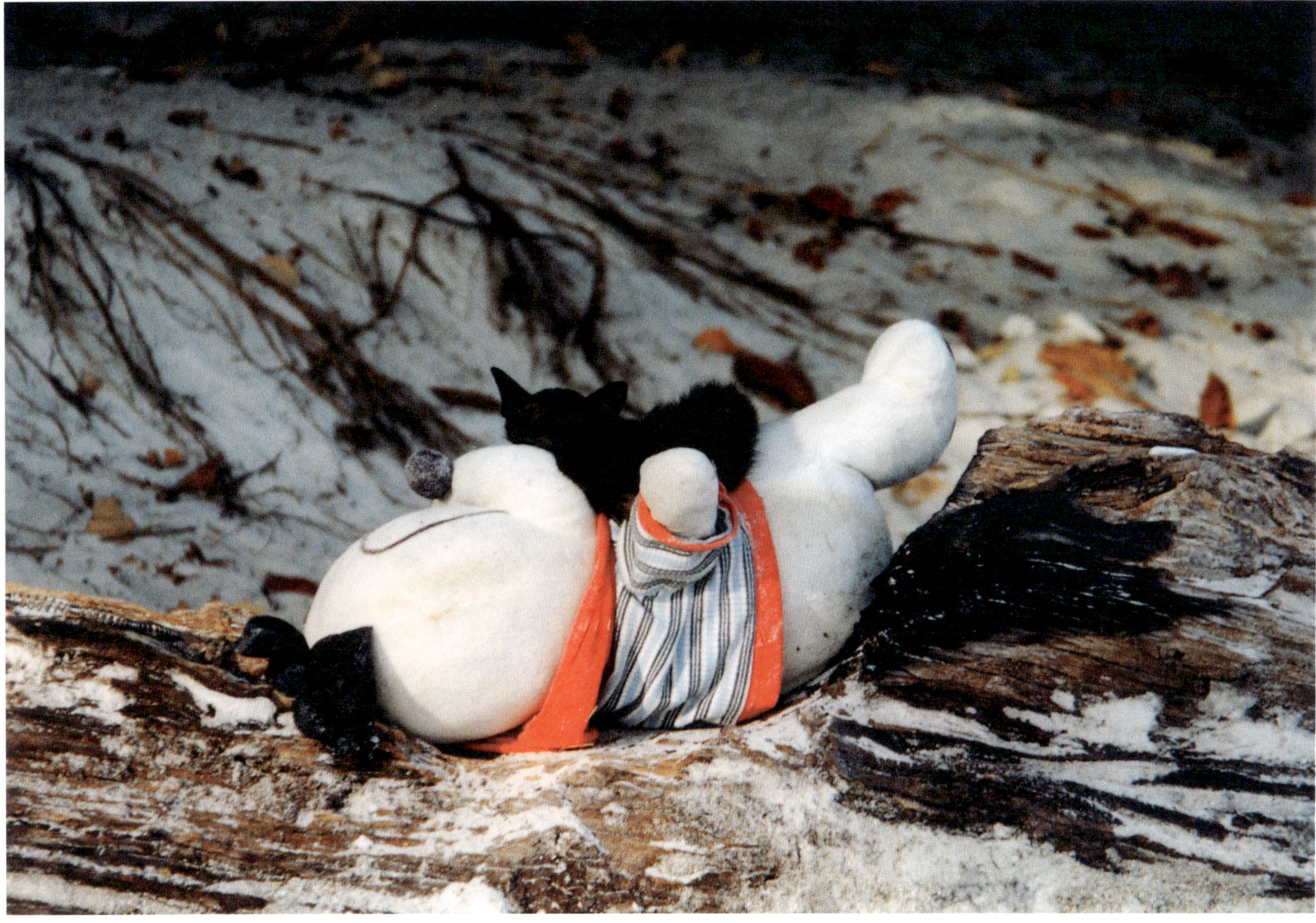

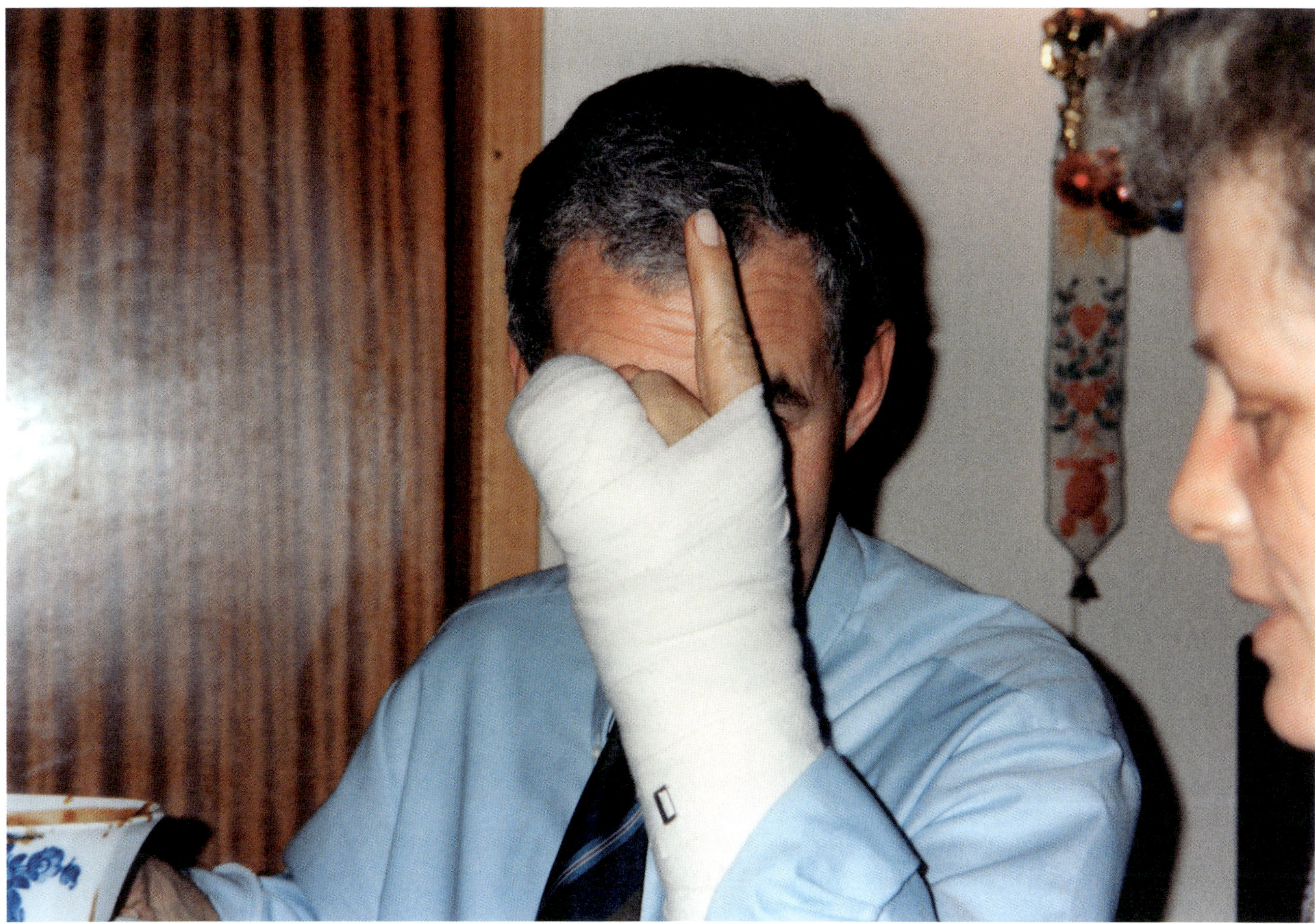

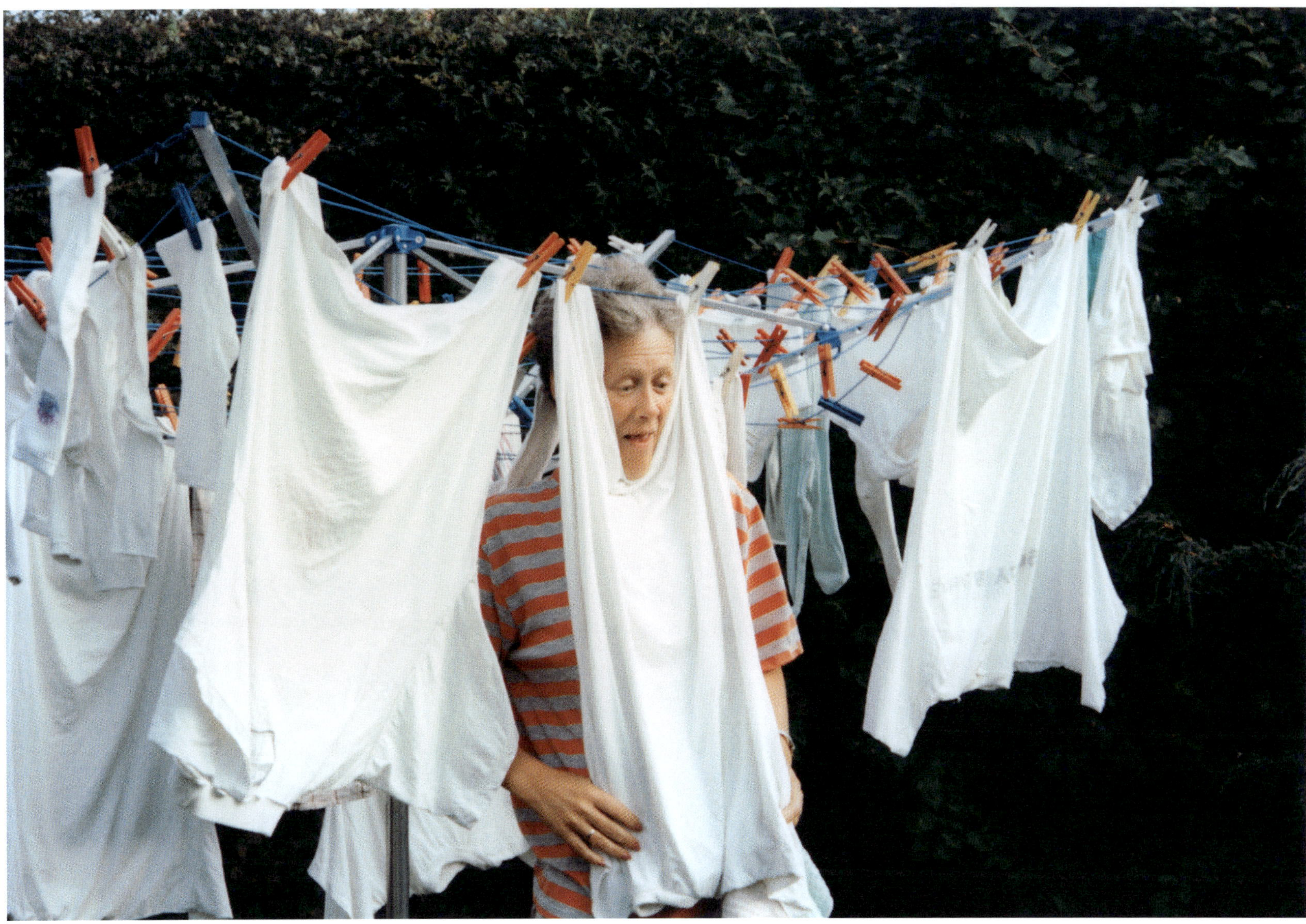

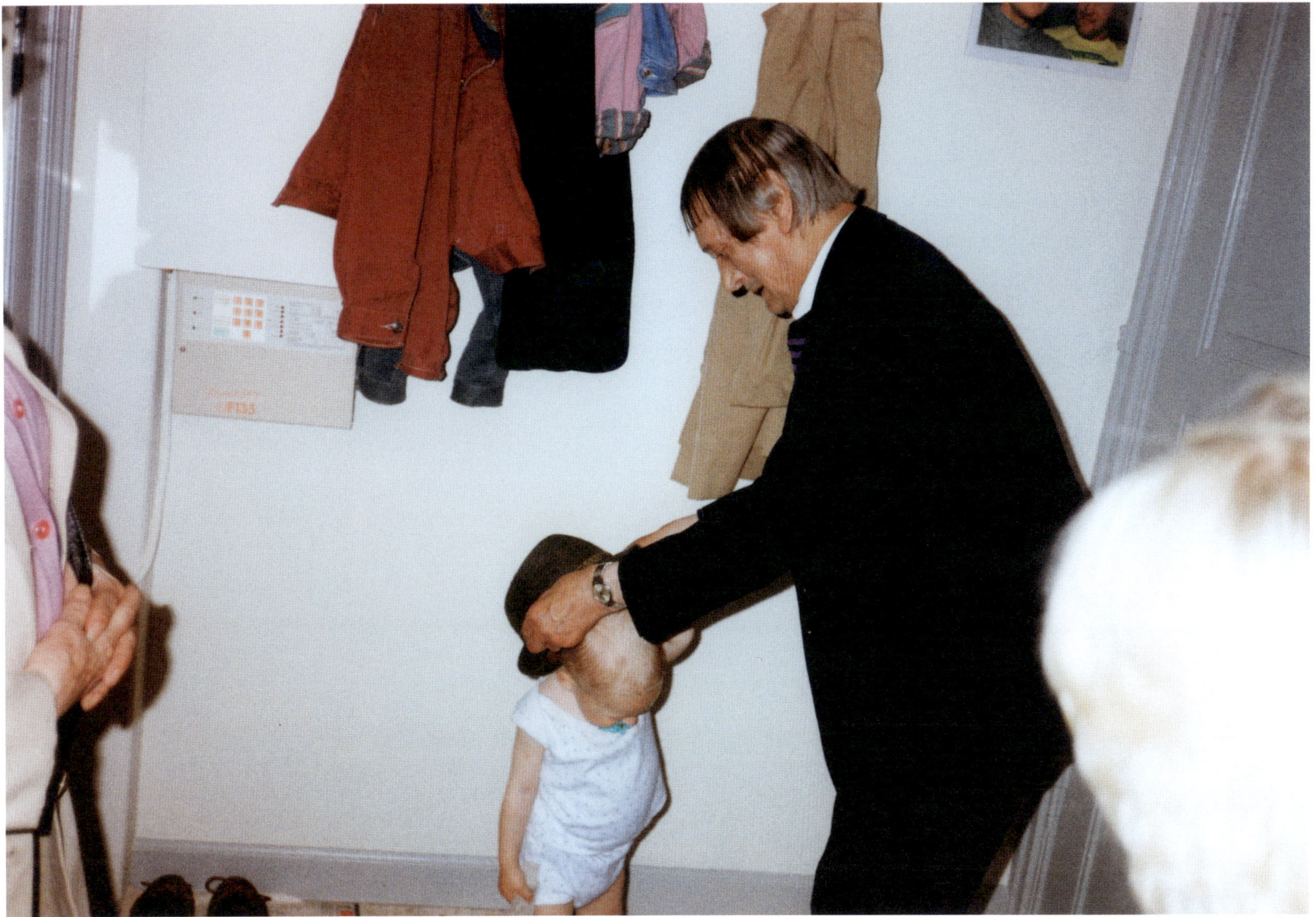

It would be strange if it wasn't like that when you are left to yourself for 24 hours a day. You do a lot of thinking about what happened and what will happen in the future.

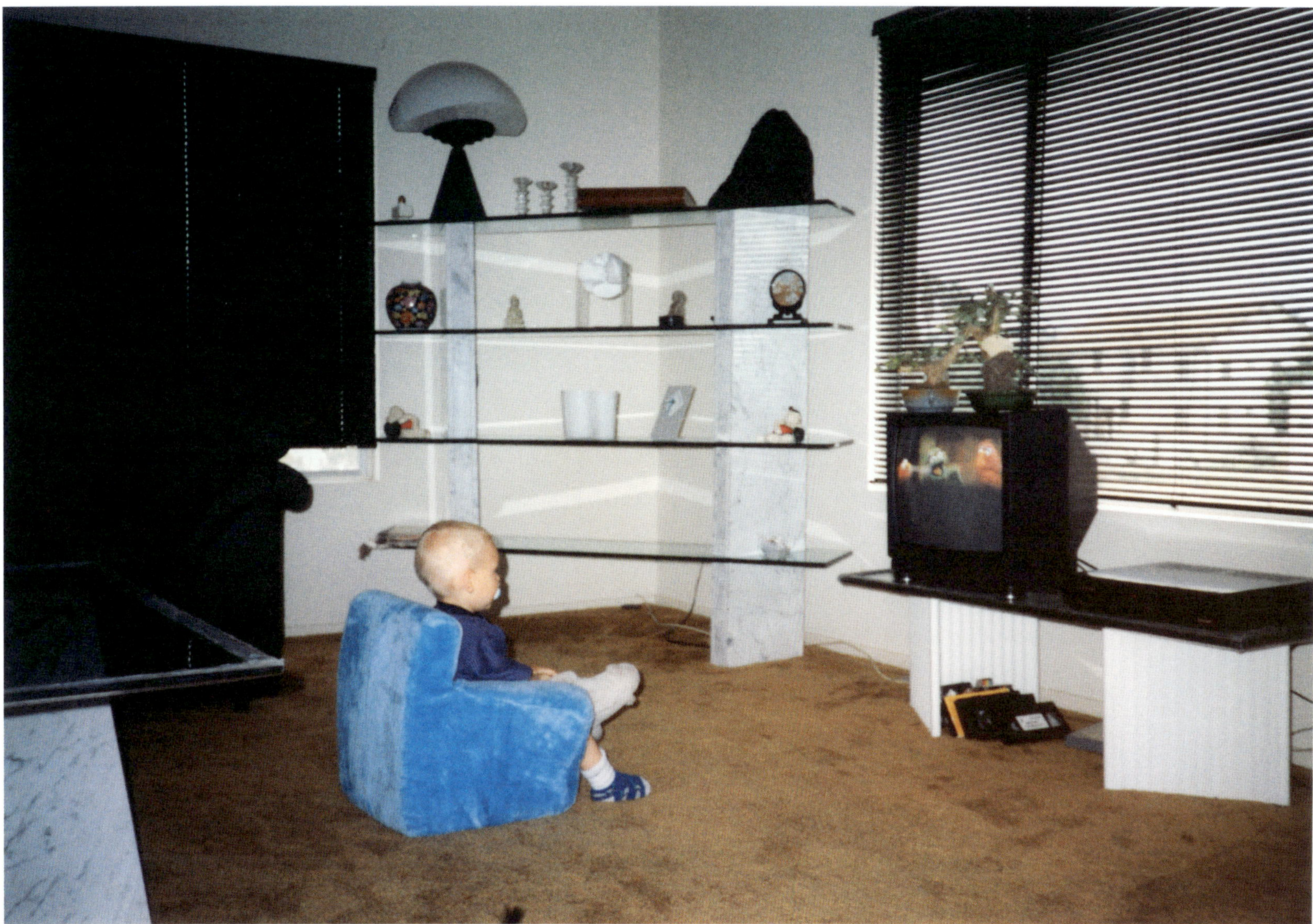

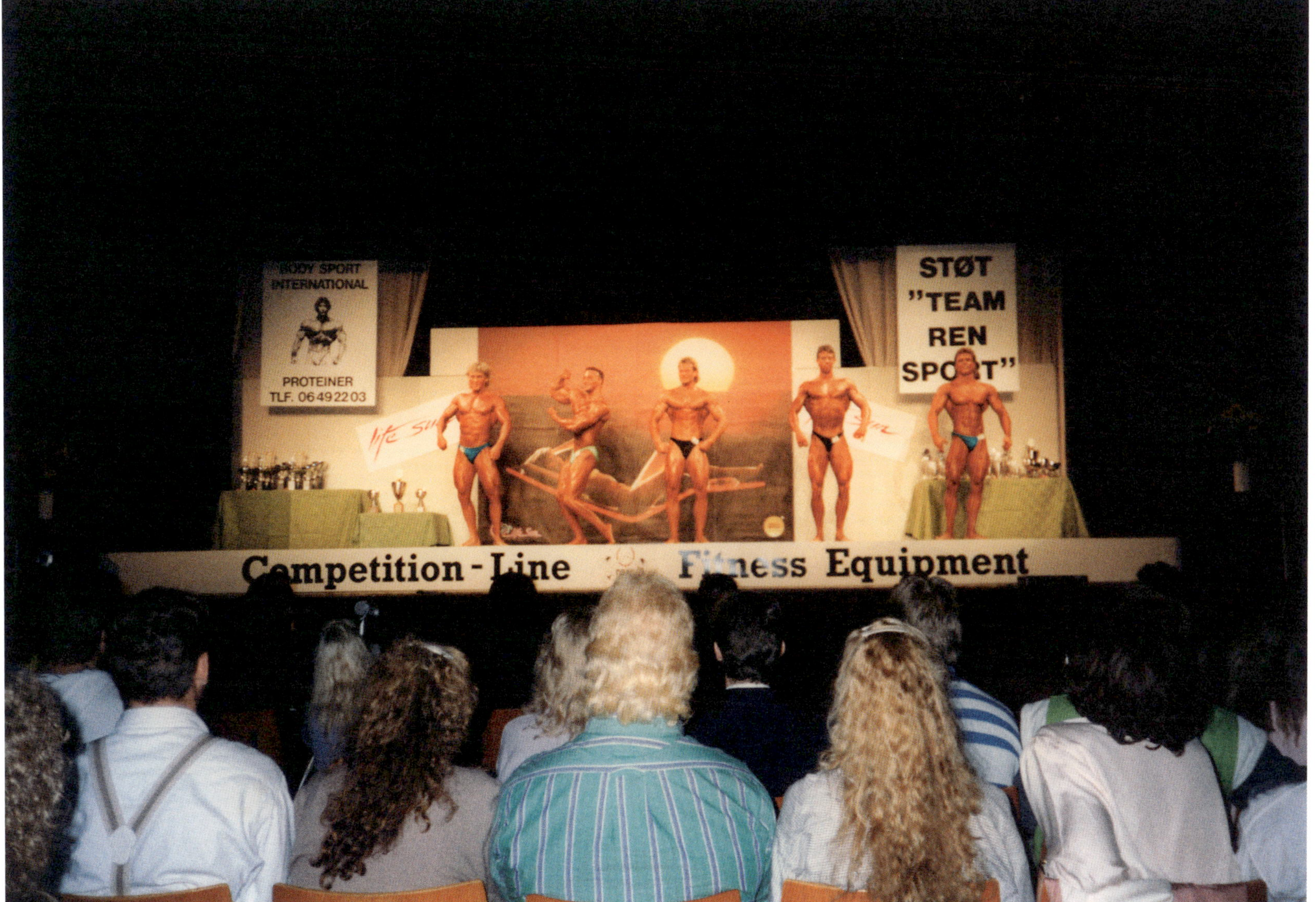
BODY SPORT
INTERNATIONAL
PROTEINER
TLF. 06 49 22 03
STØT
"TEAM
REN
SPORT"
Competition - Line   Fitness Equipment

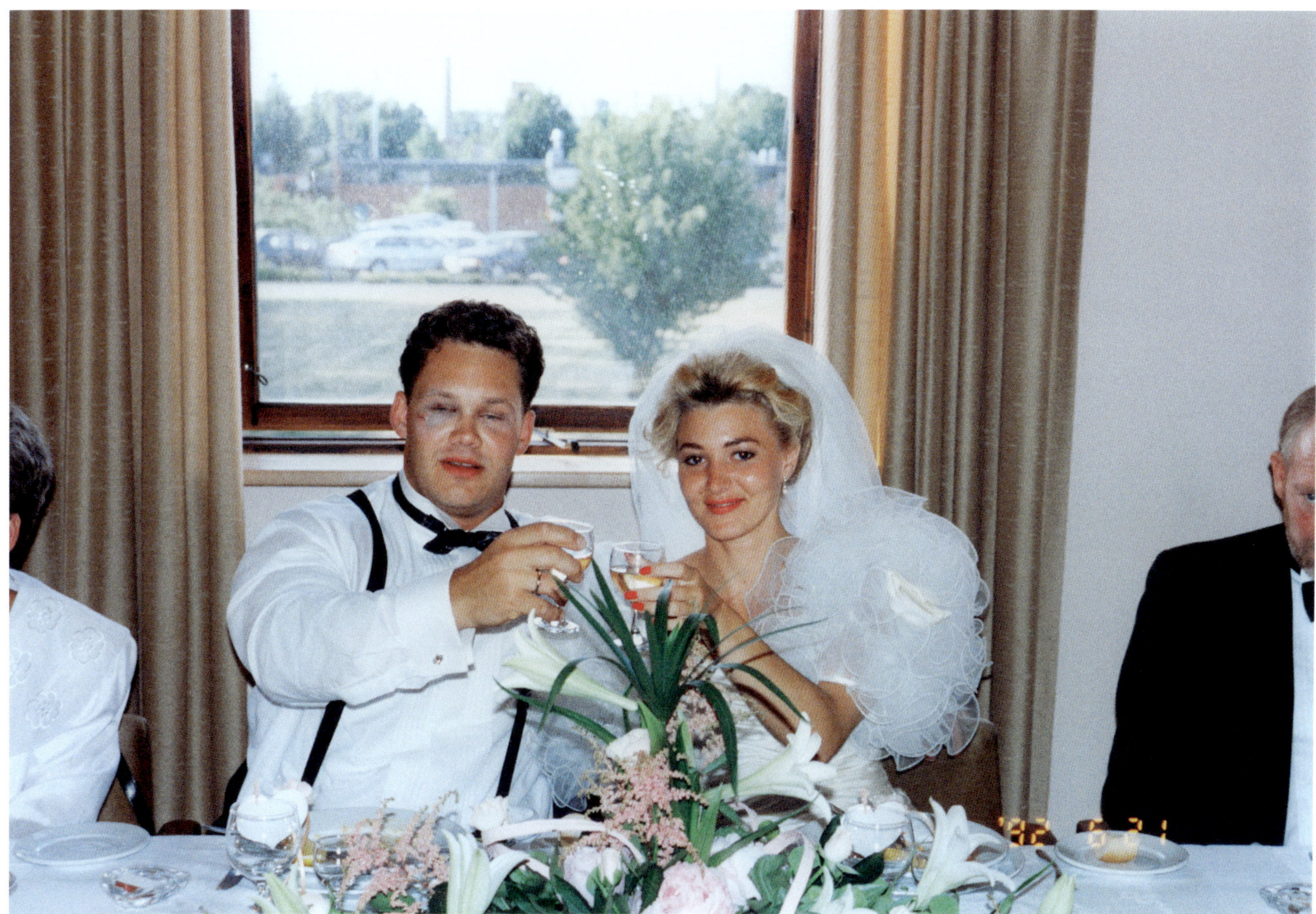

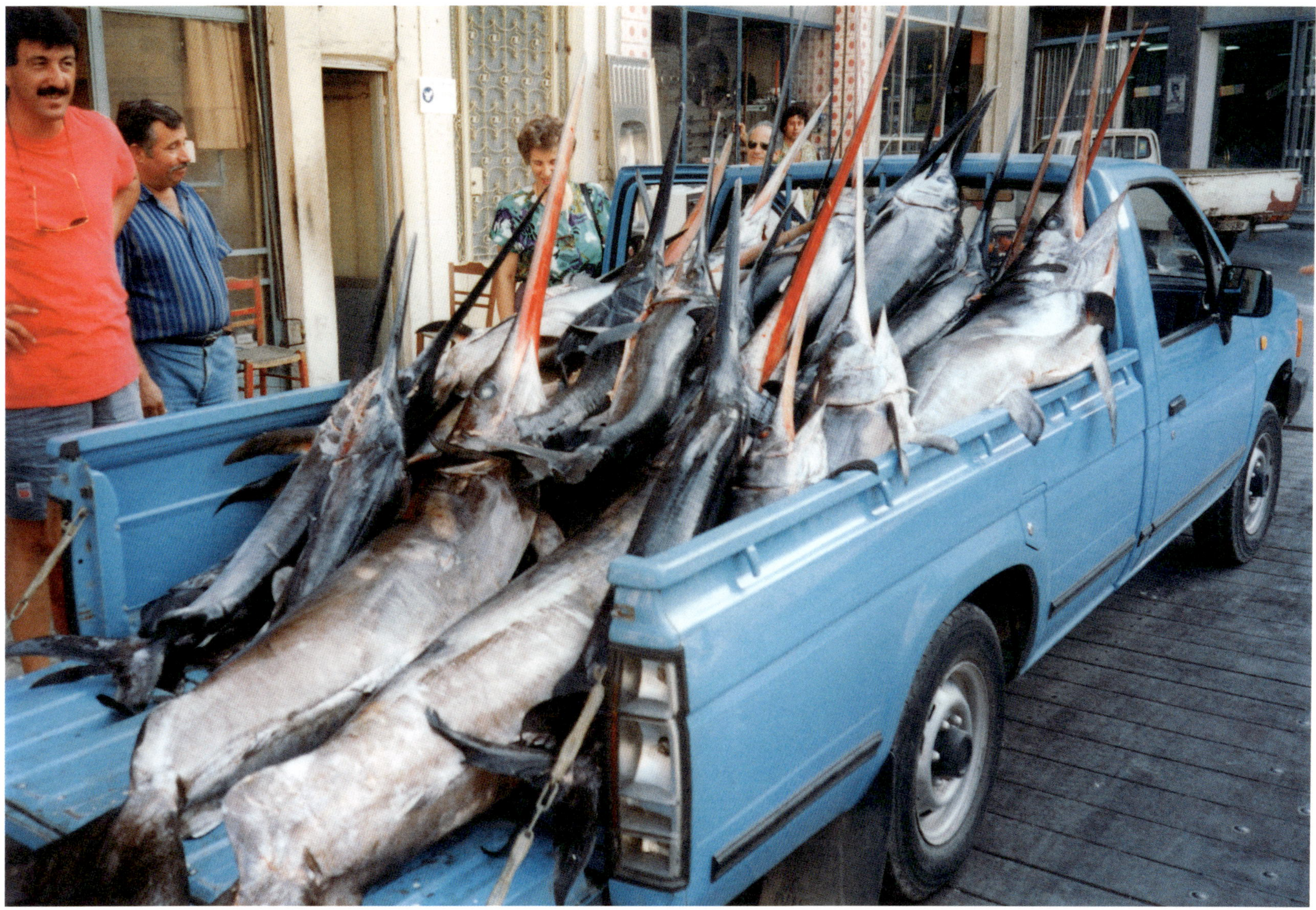

As for the mood, it is up and Down. One moment you are high up and it all seems manageable. The next moment you are down all the way to the basement.

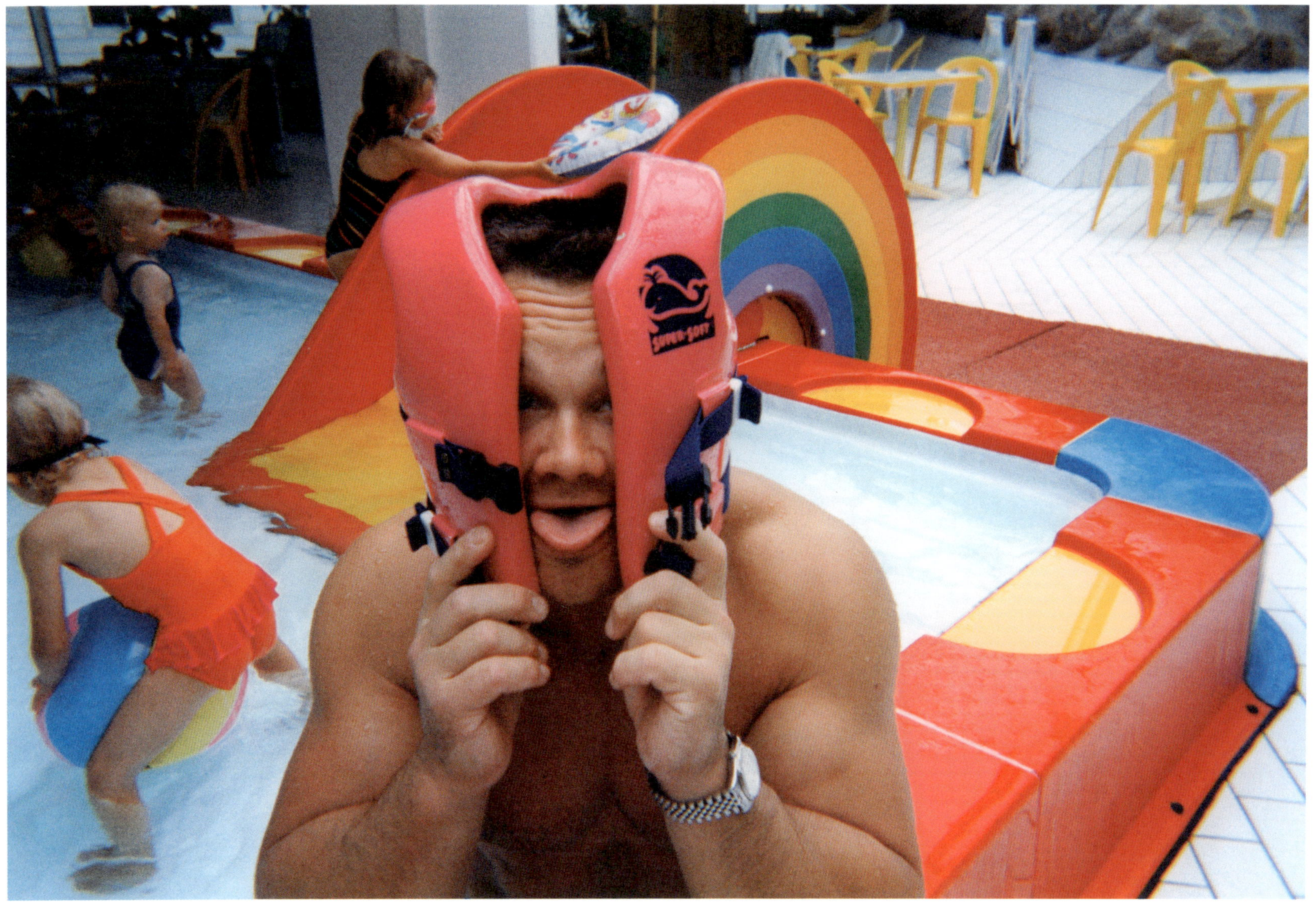

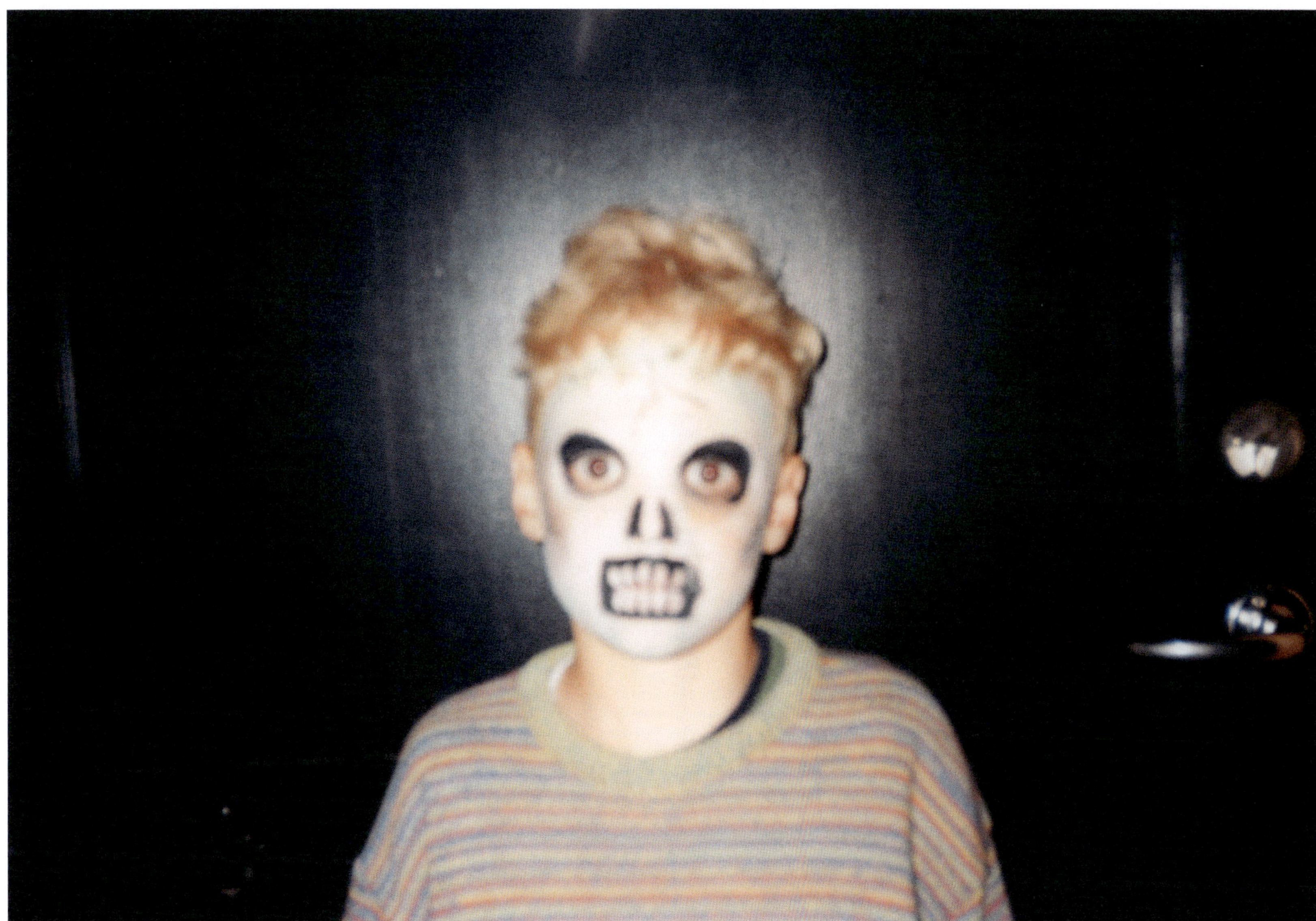

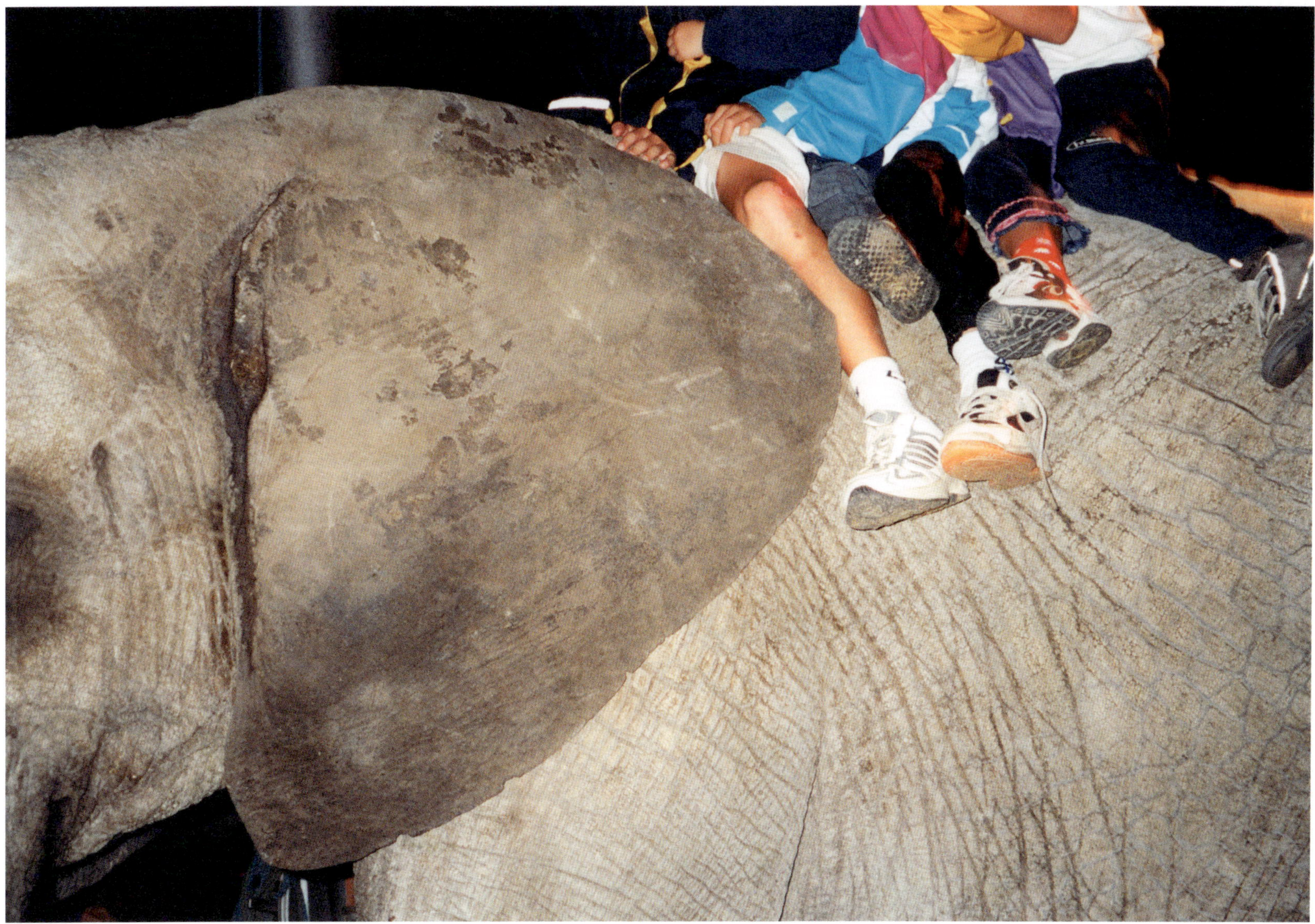

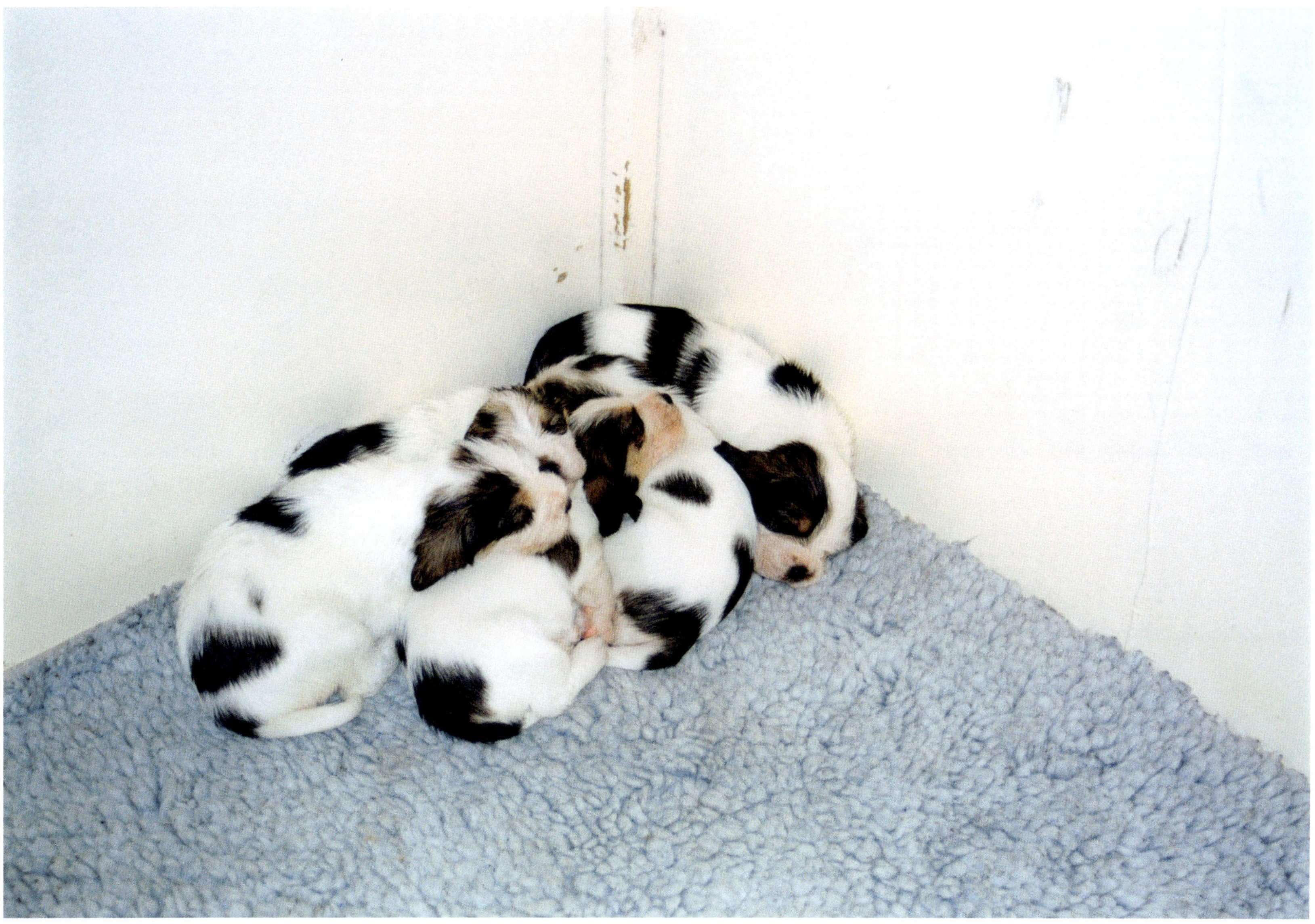

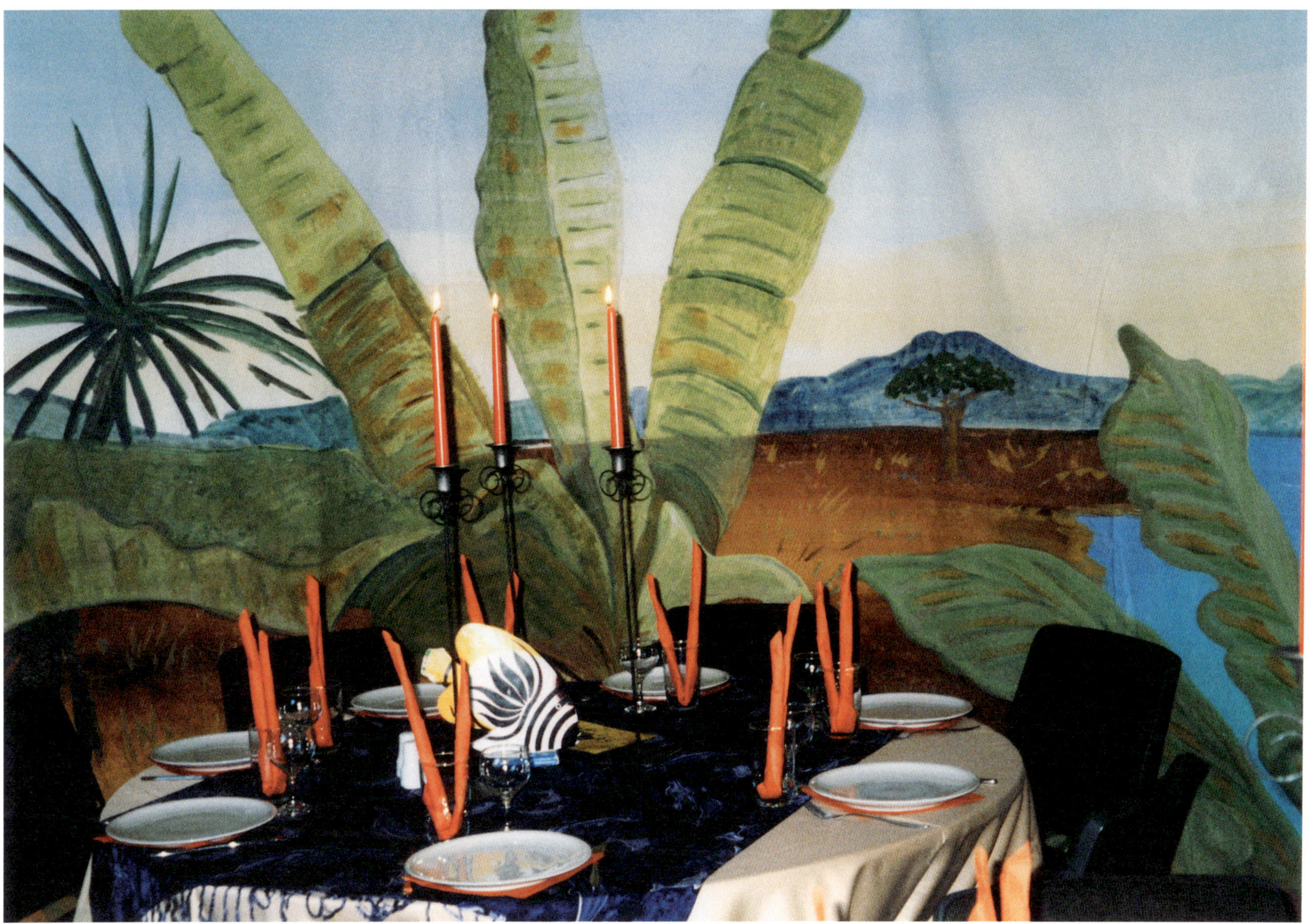

You said Luna wakes and calls at night,

that's probably only a small part of the big

price we all have to pay for my mistakes.

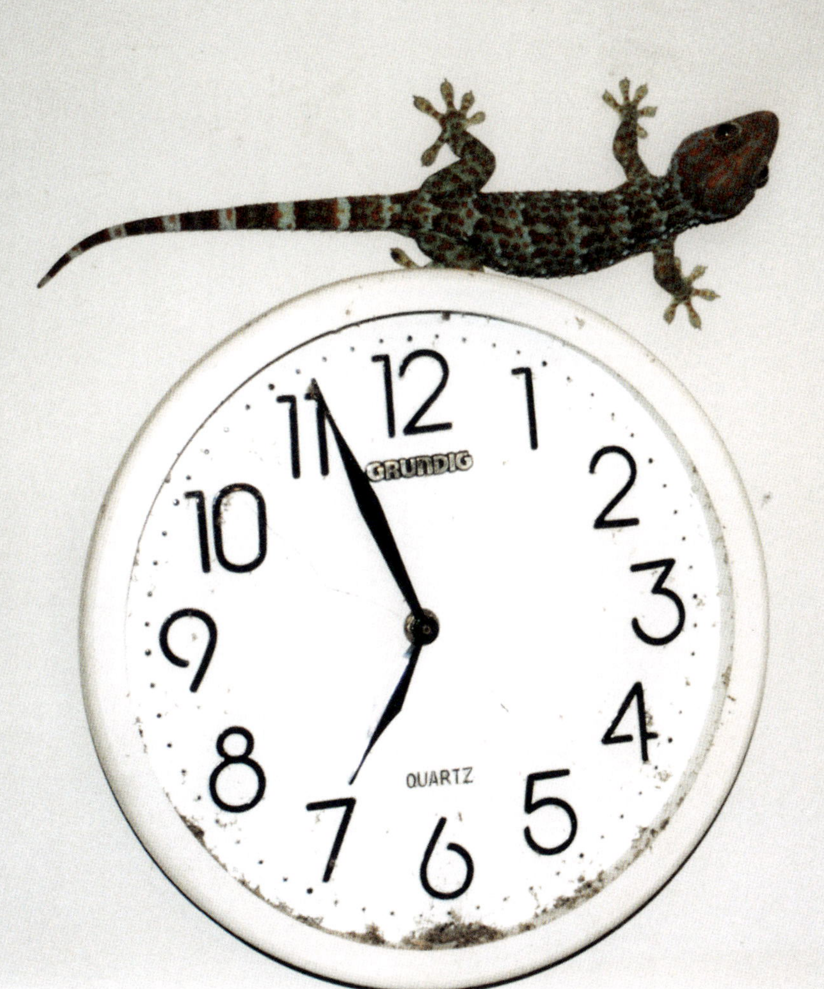
GRUNDIG
QUARTZ
12
1
2
3
4
5
6
7
8
9
10
11

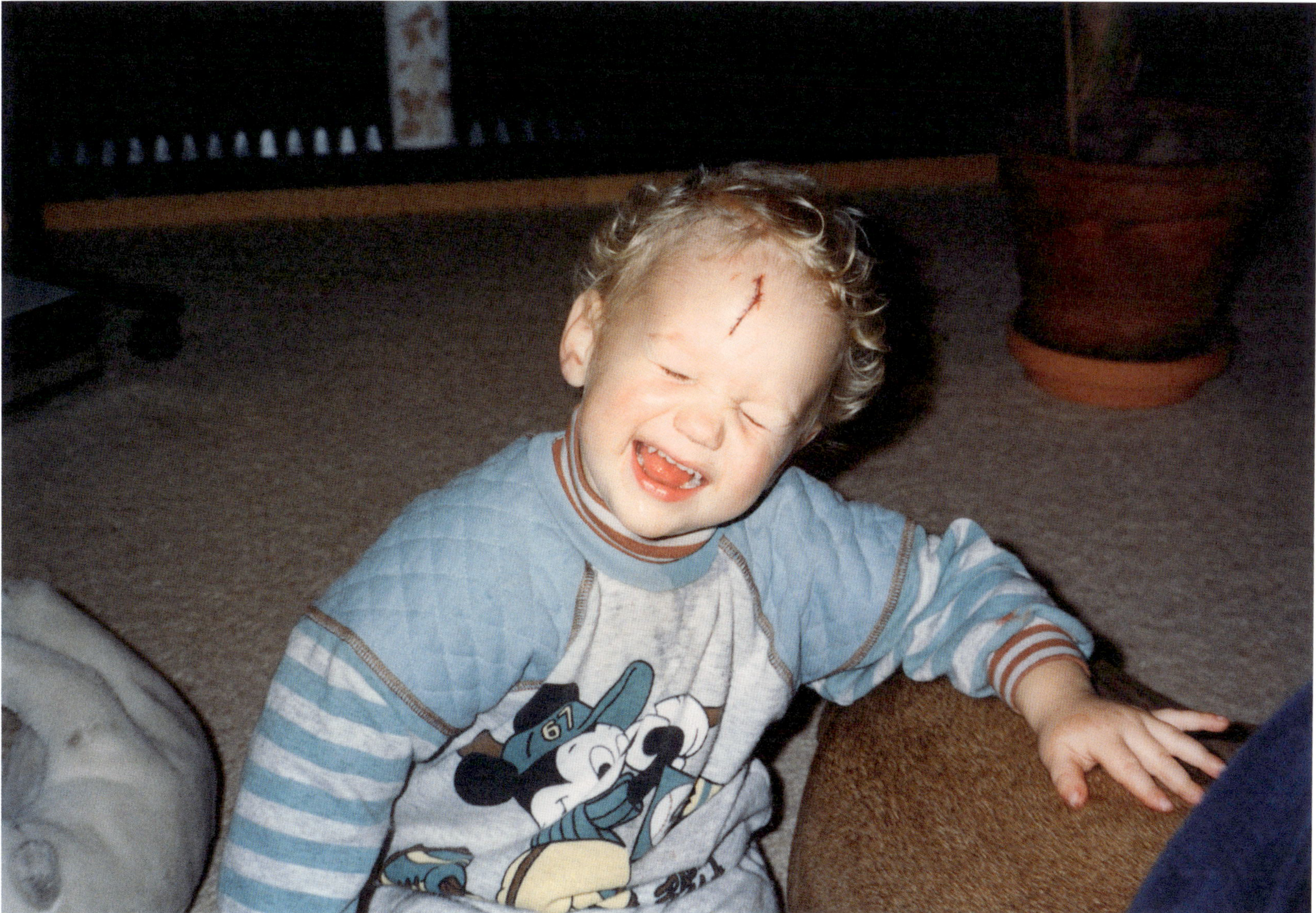

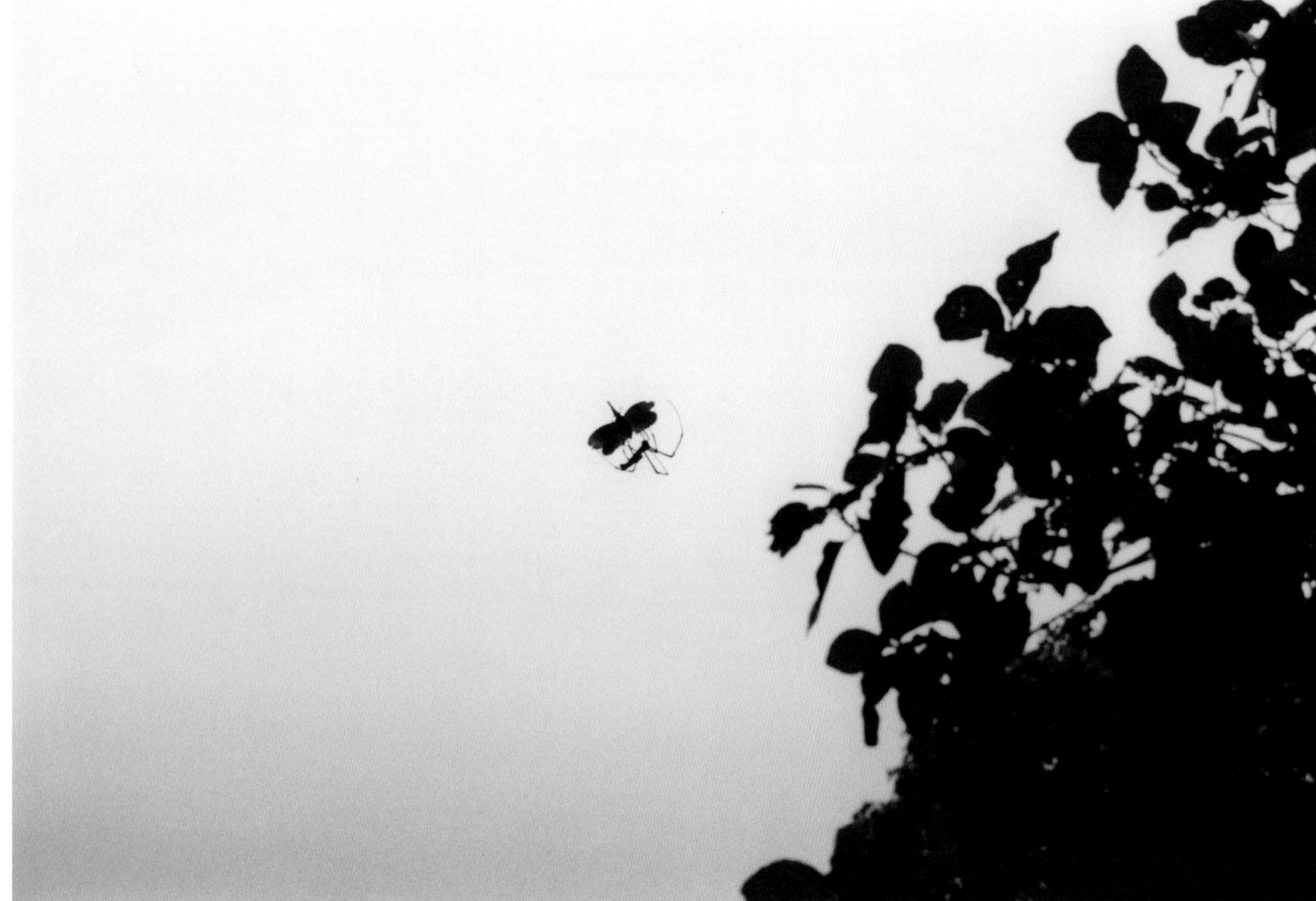

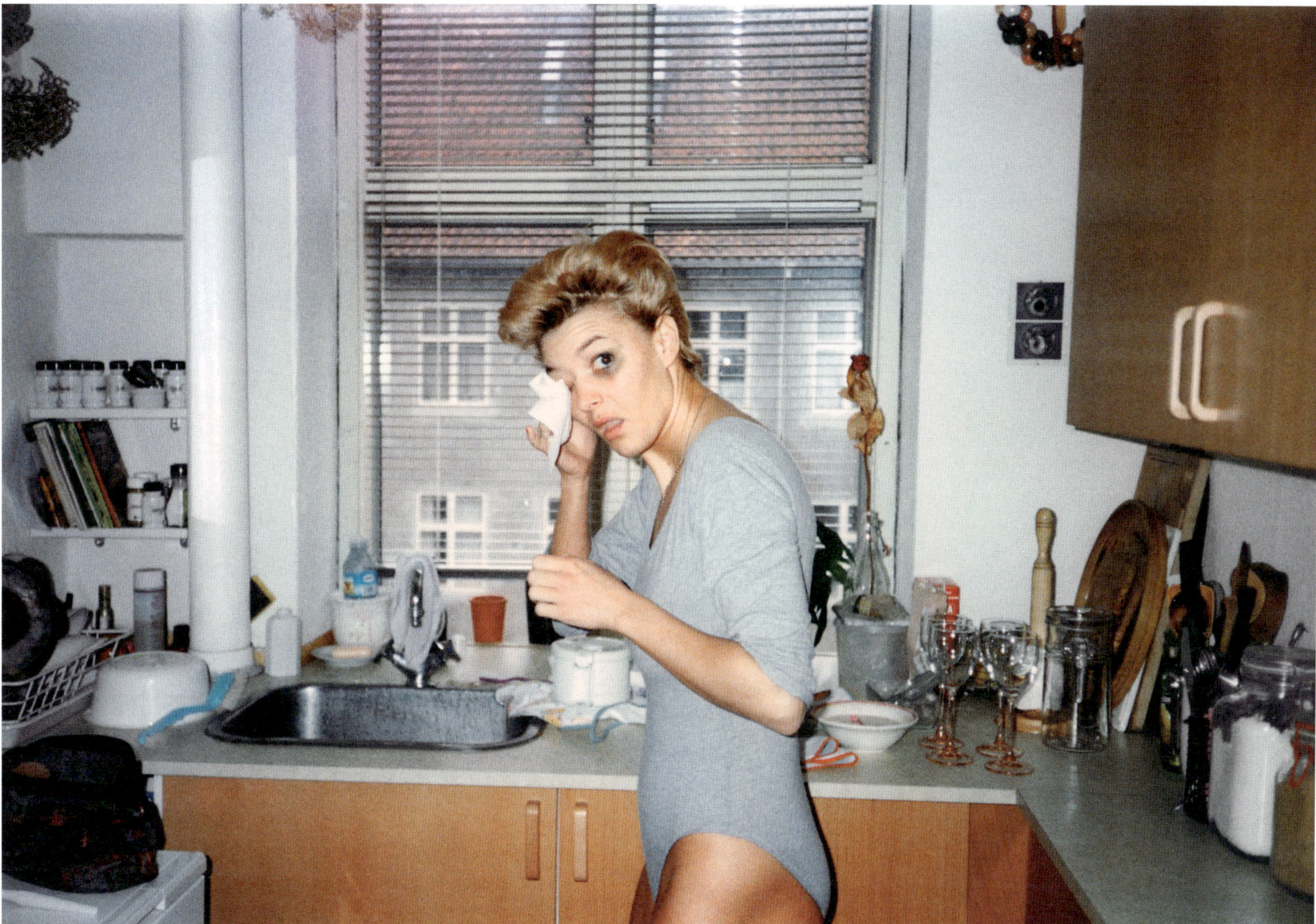

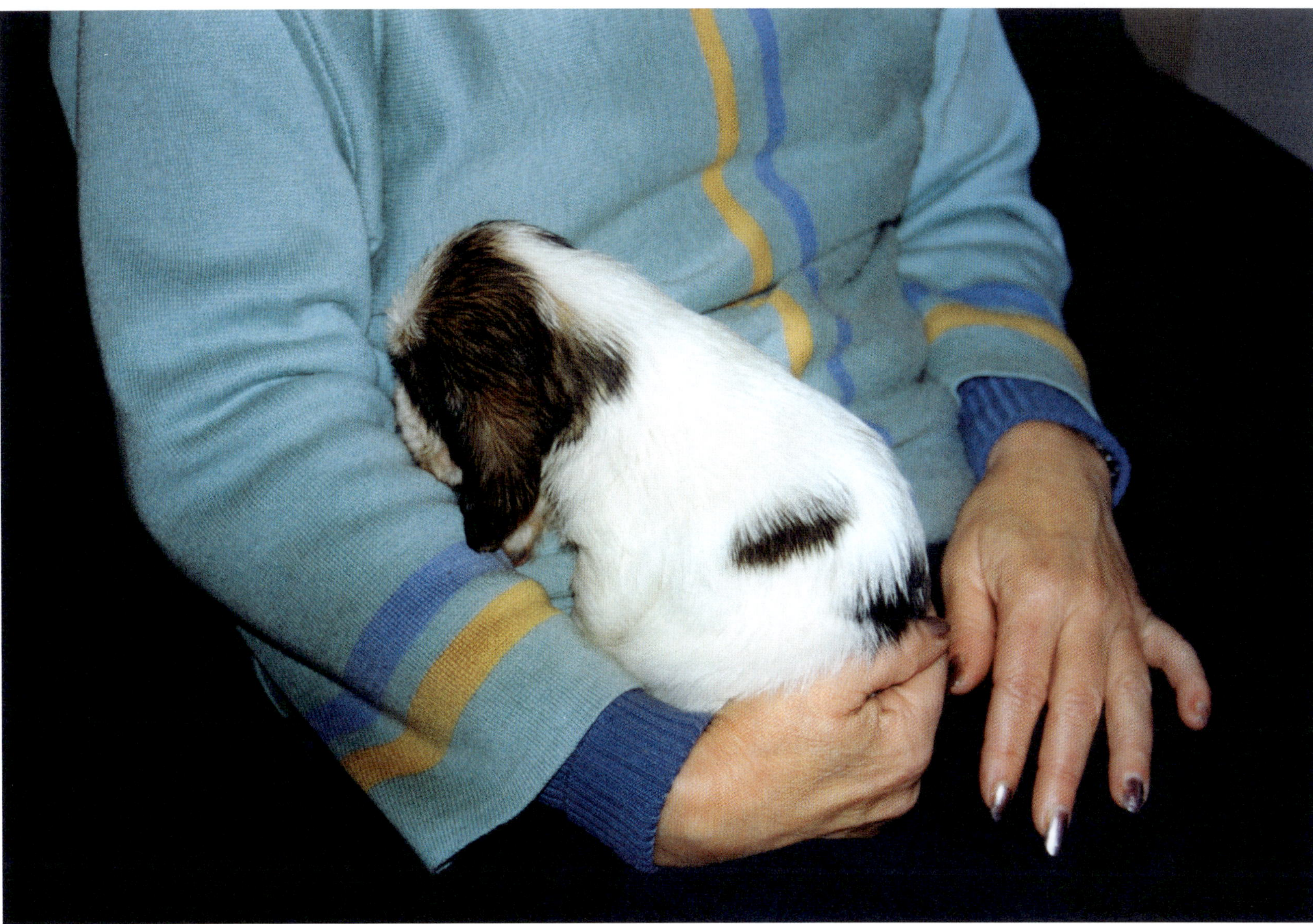

Although our situation is not currently the most positive, you are still allowed to dream.

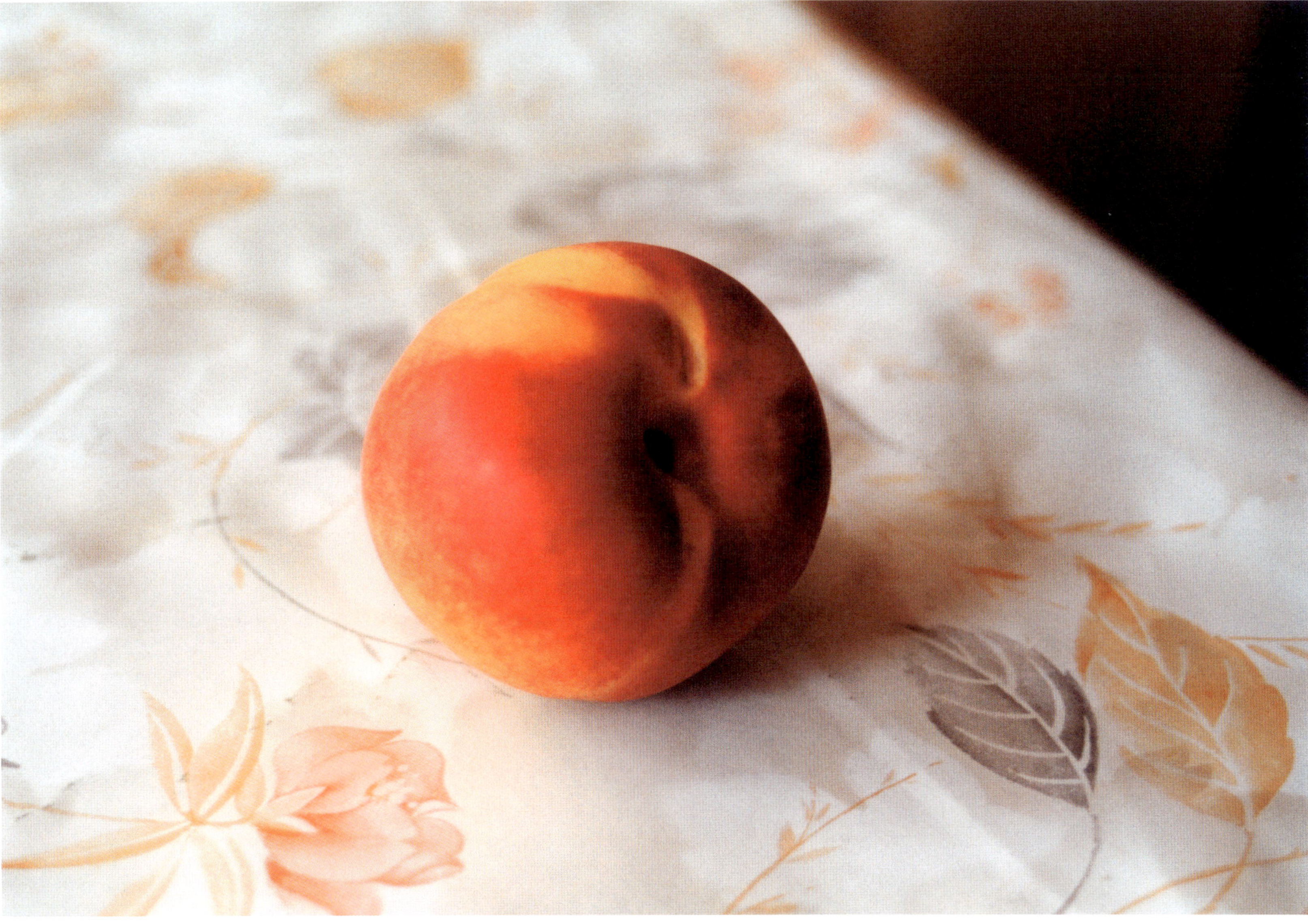

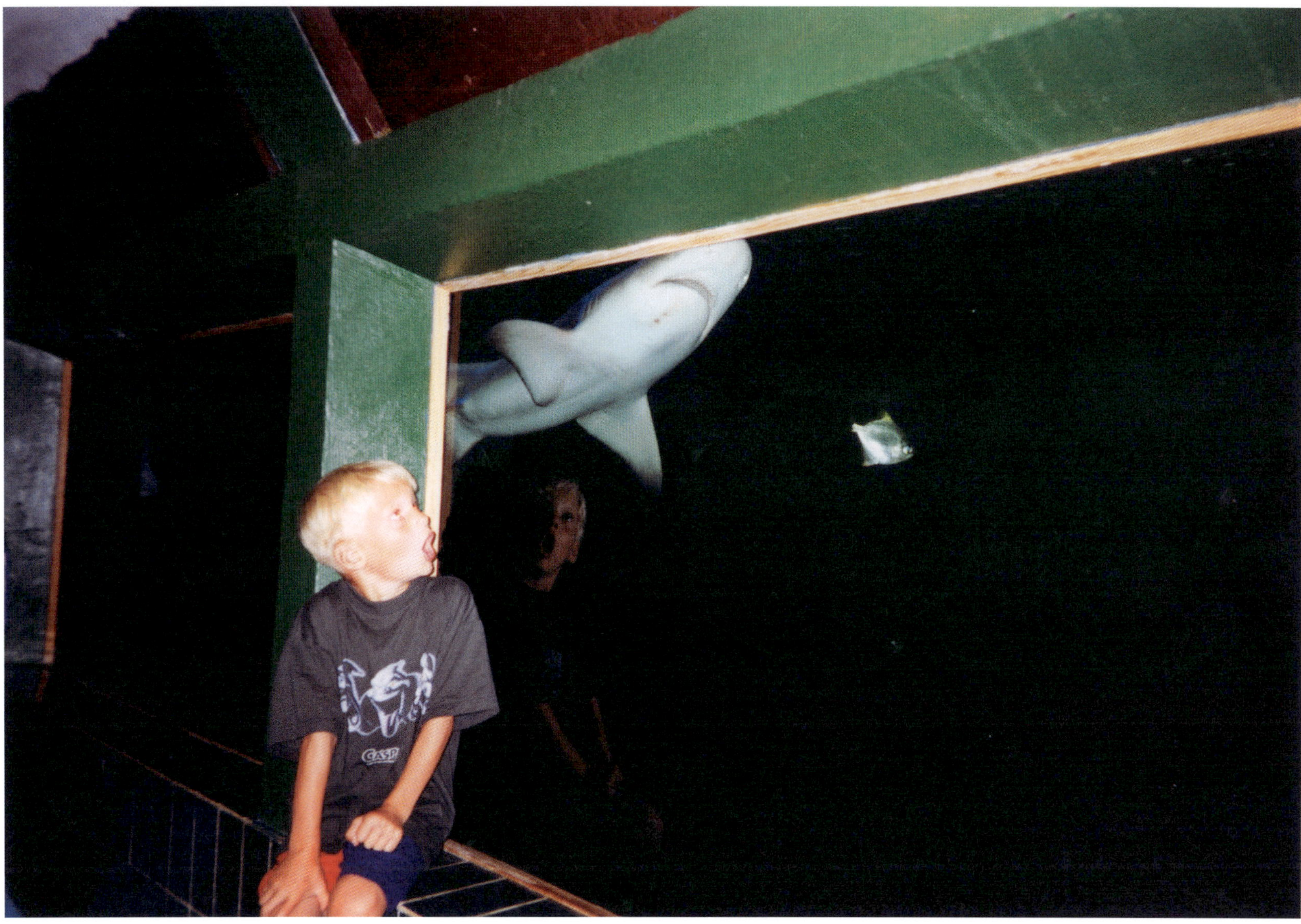

Something you can be sure of is that

there's lots of surprises waiting for you.

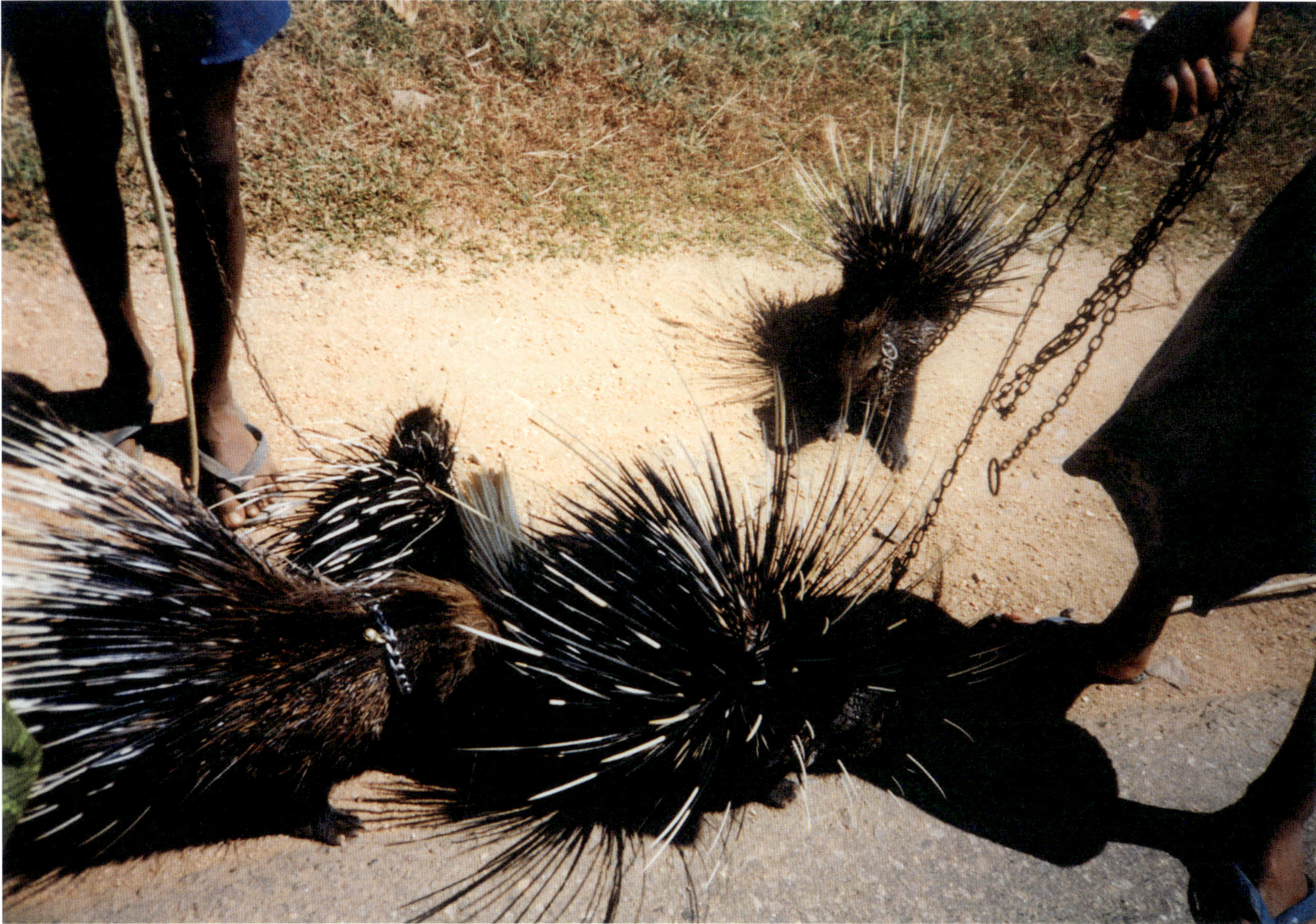

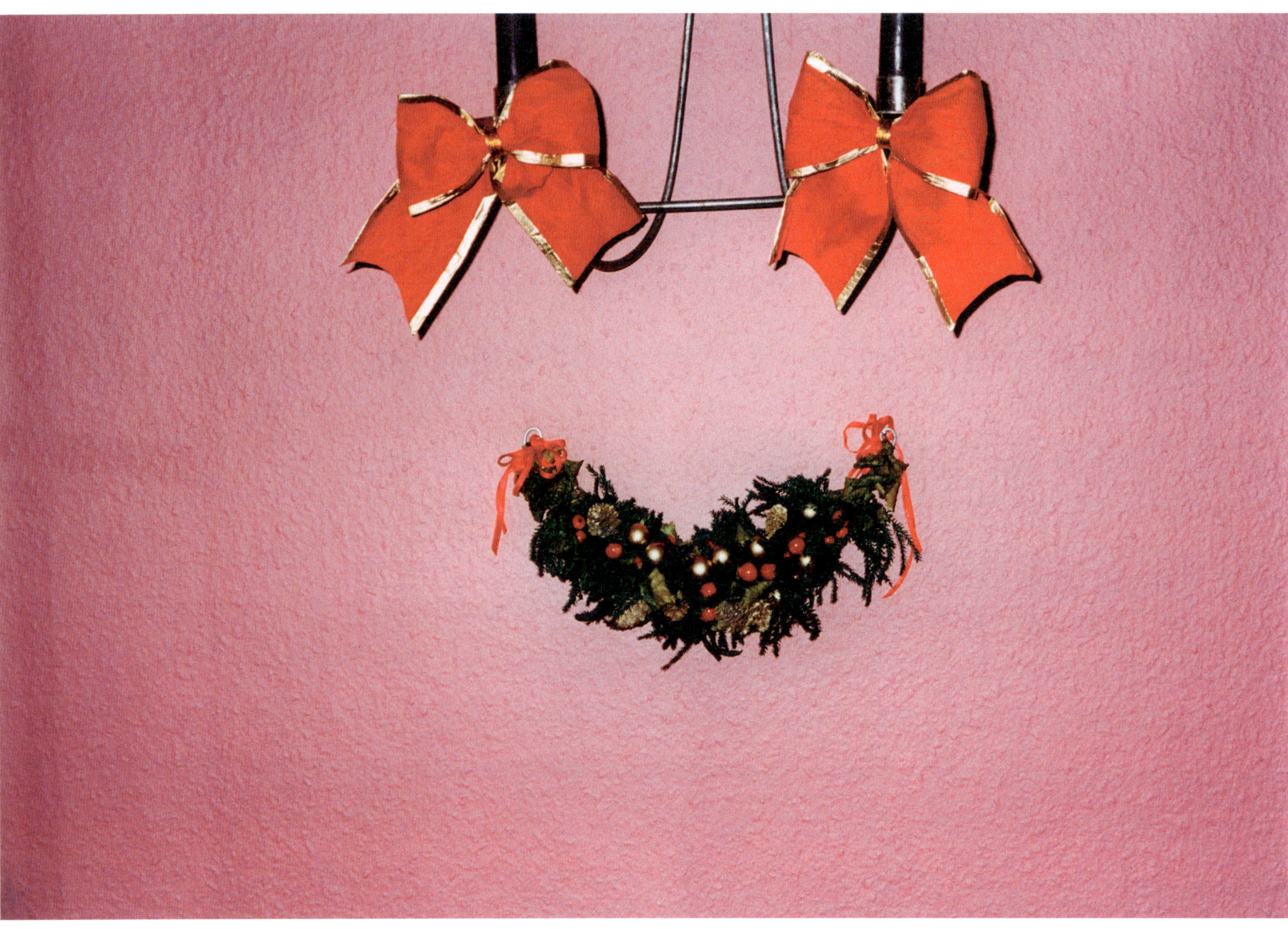

you're going to take a helicopter ride one day

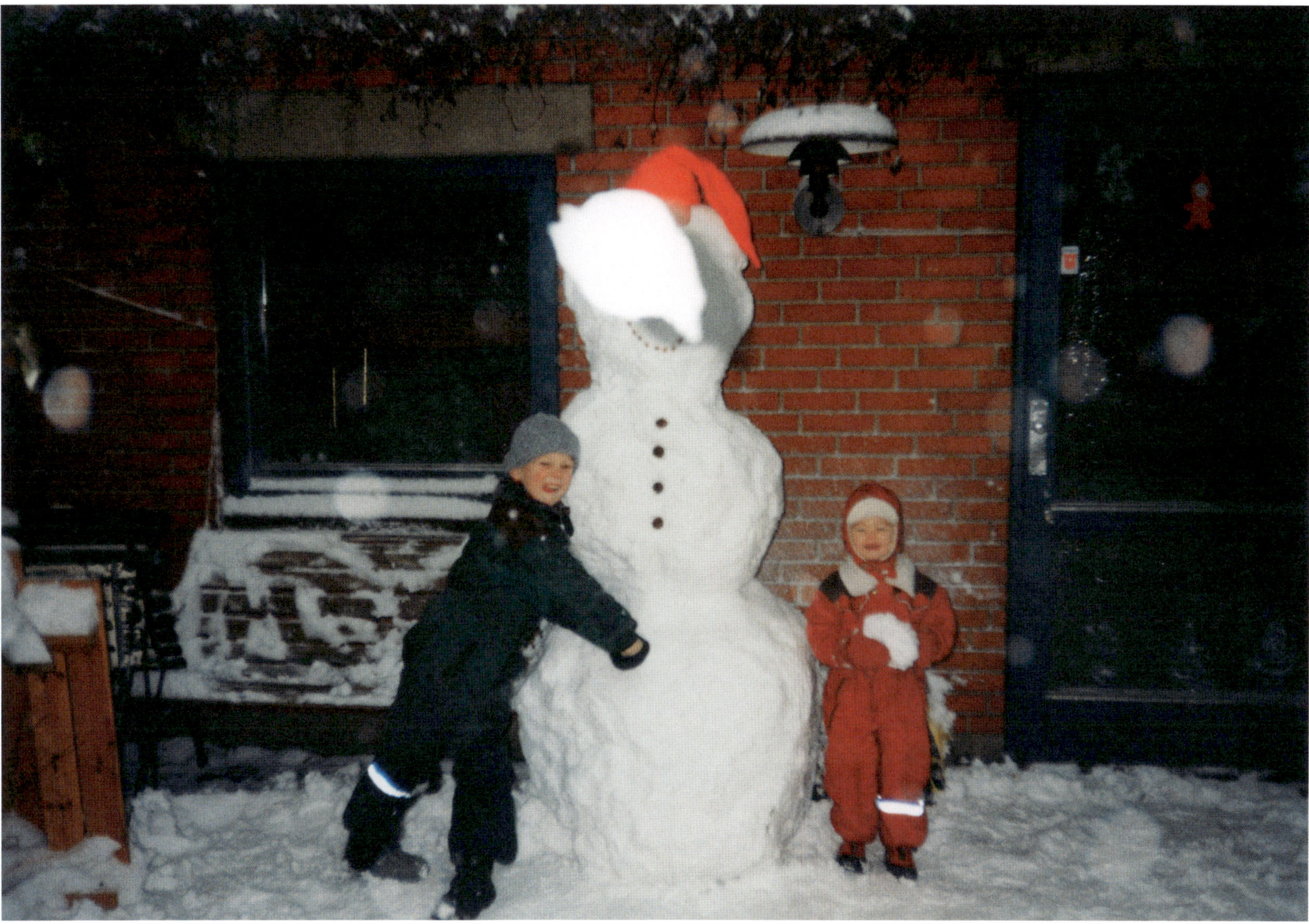

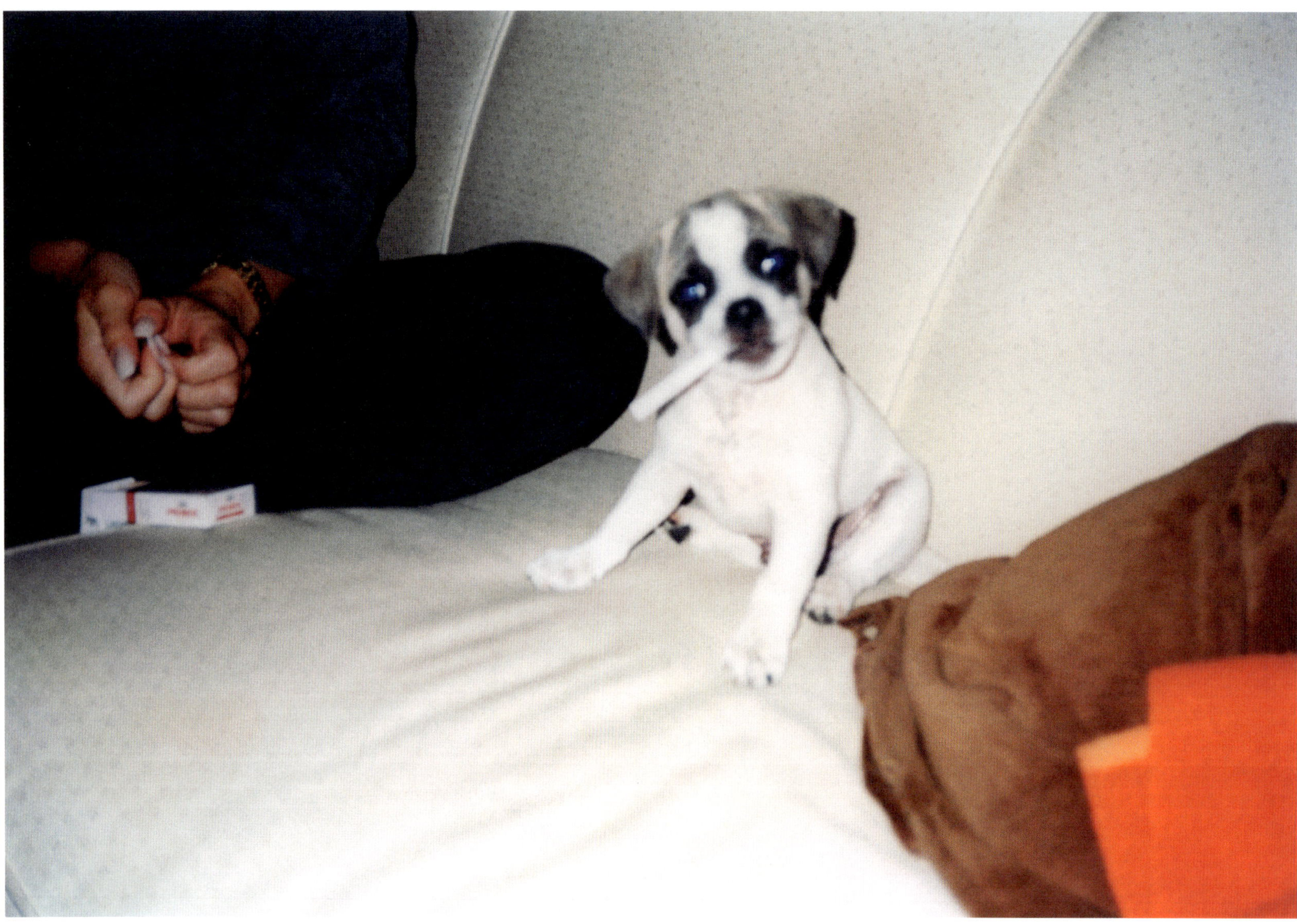

and after go swimming with dolphins.

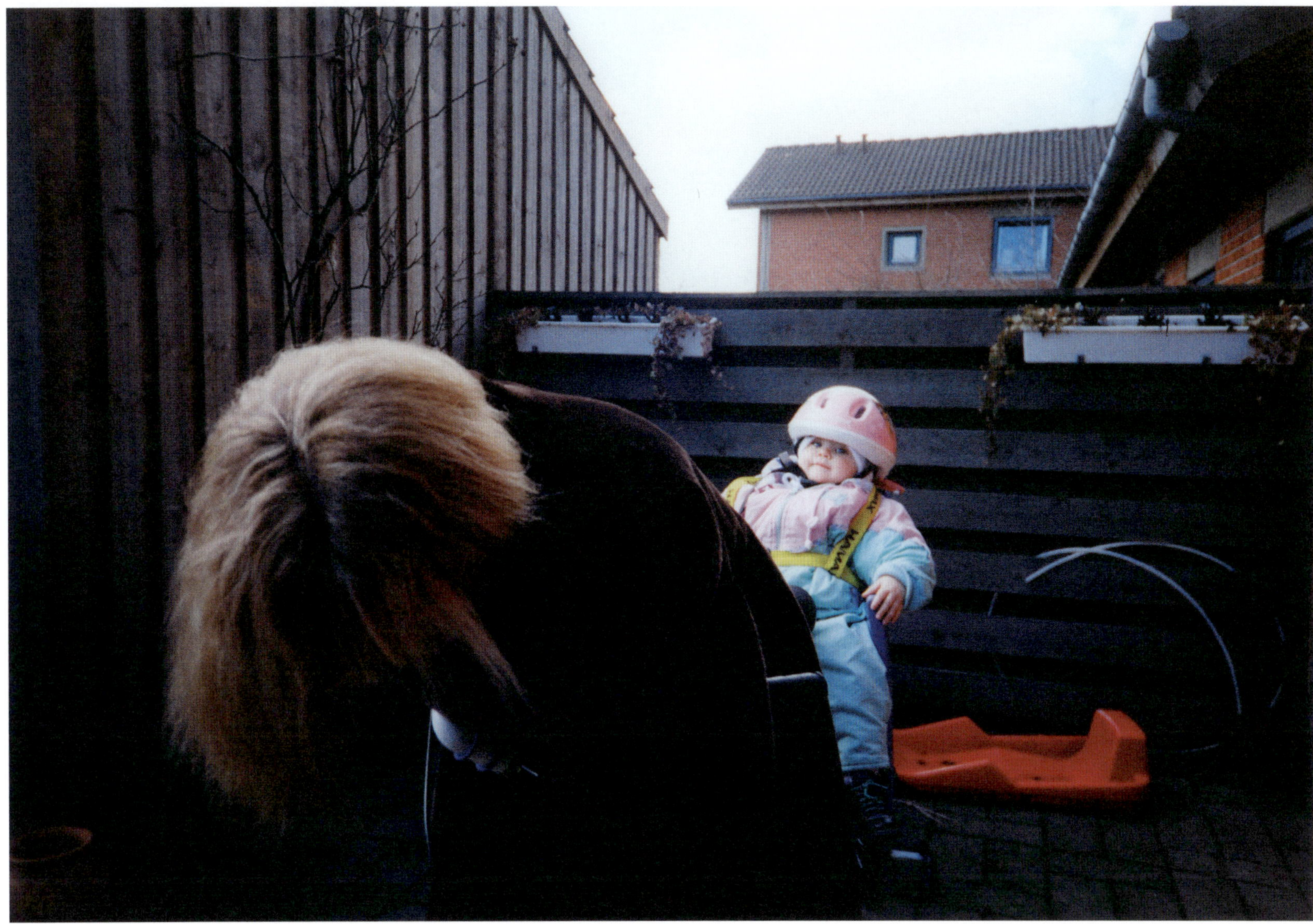

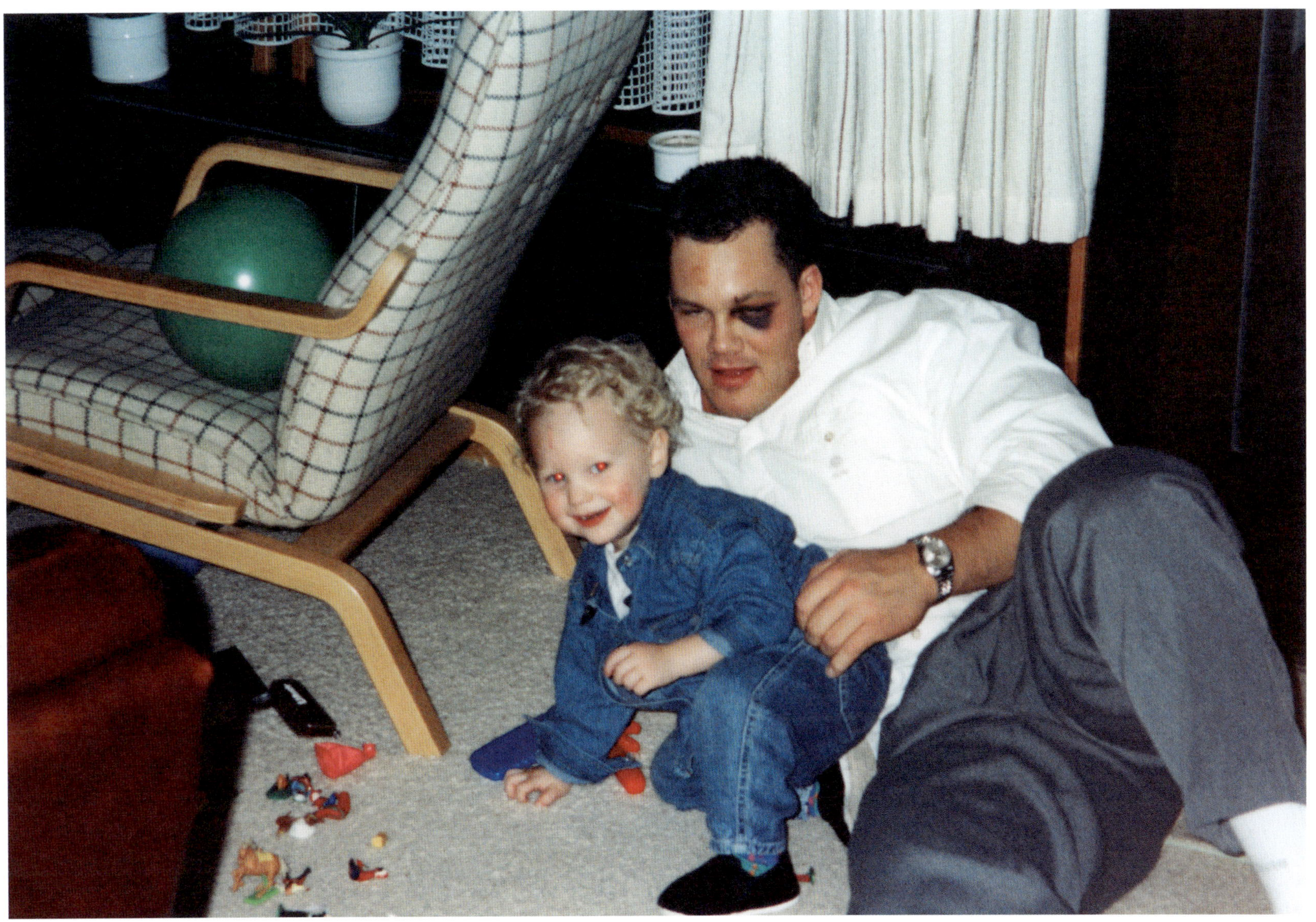

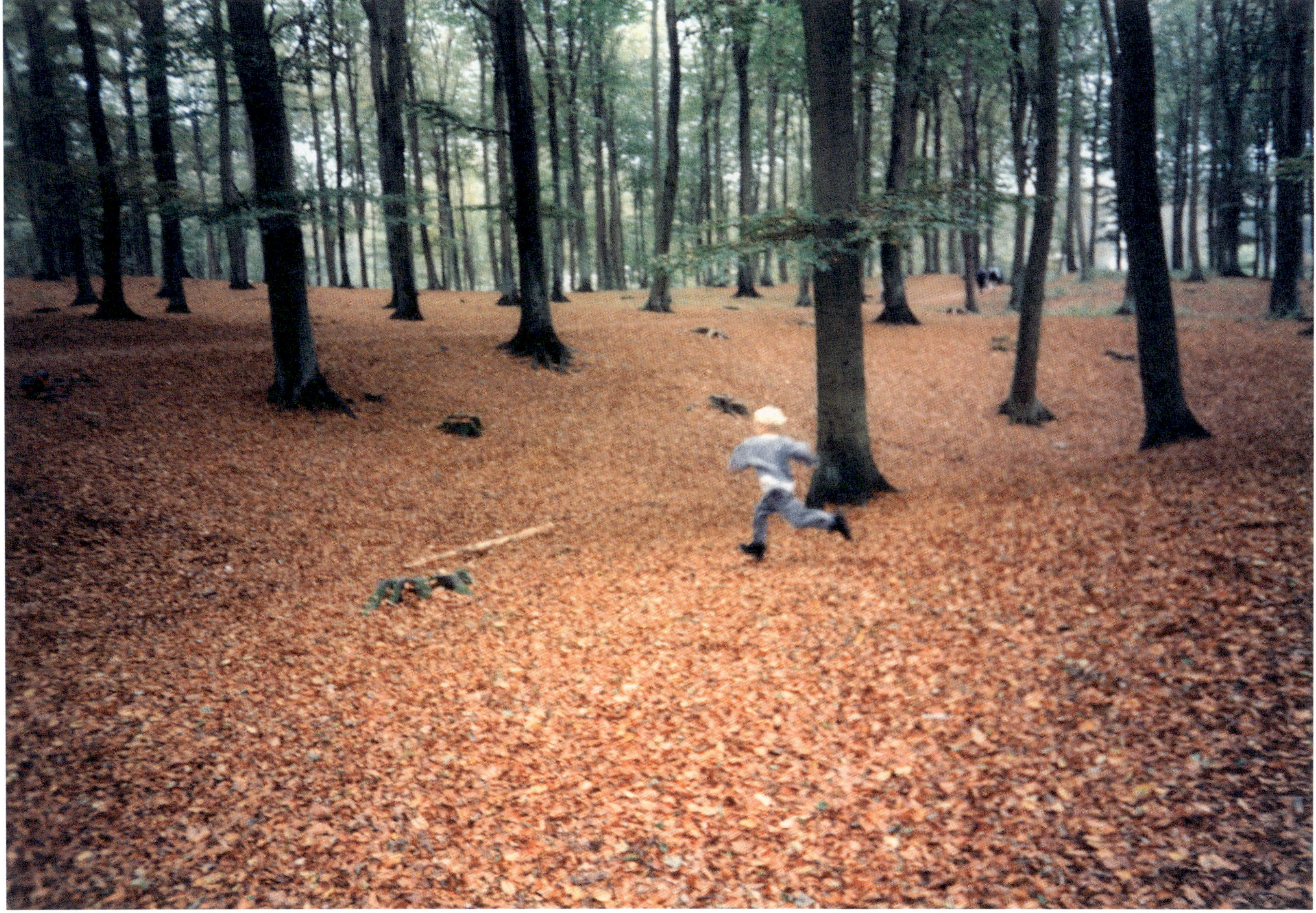

Now I want to end with a quote by Camus.

"Prison does not evoke reconciliation. Long-term confinement breeds either lackeys or killers, sometimes both being united in the same person"

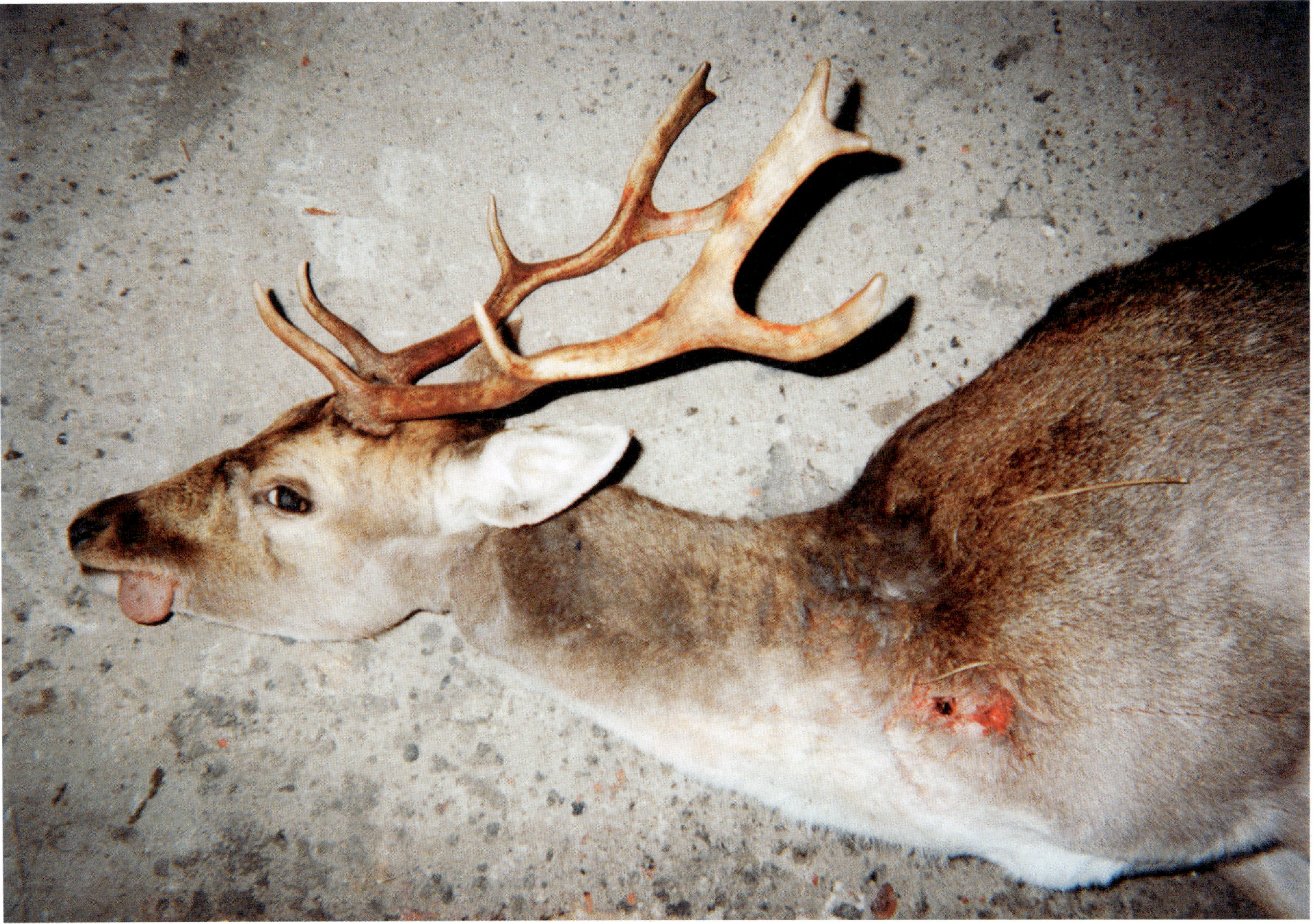

That's all for now, the Prison guard is about to Rip the letter out of my hand.

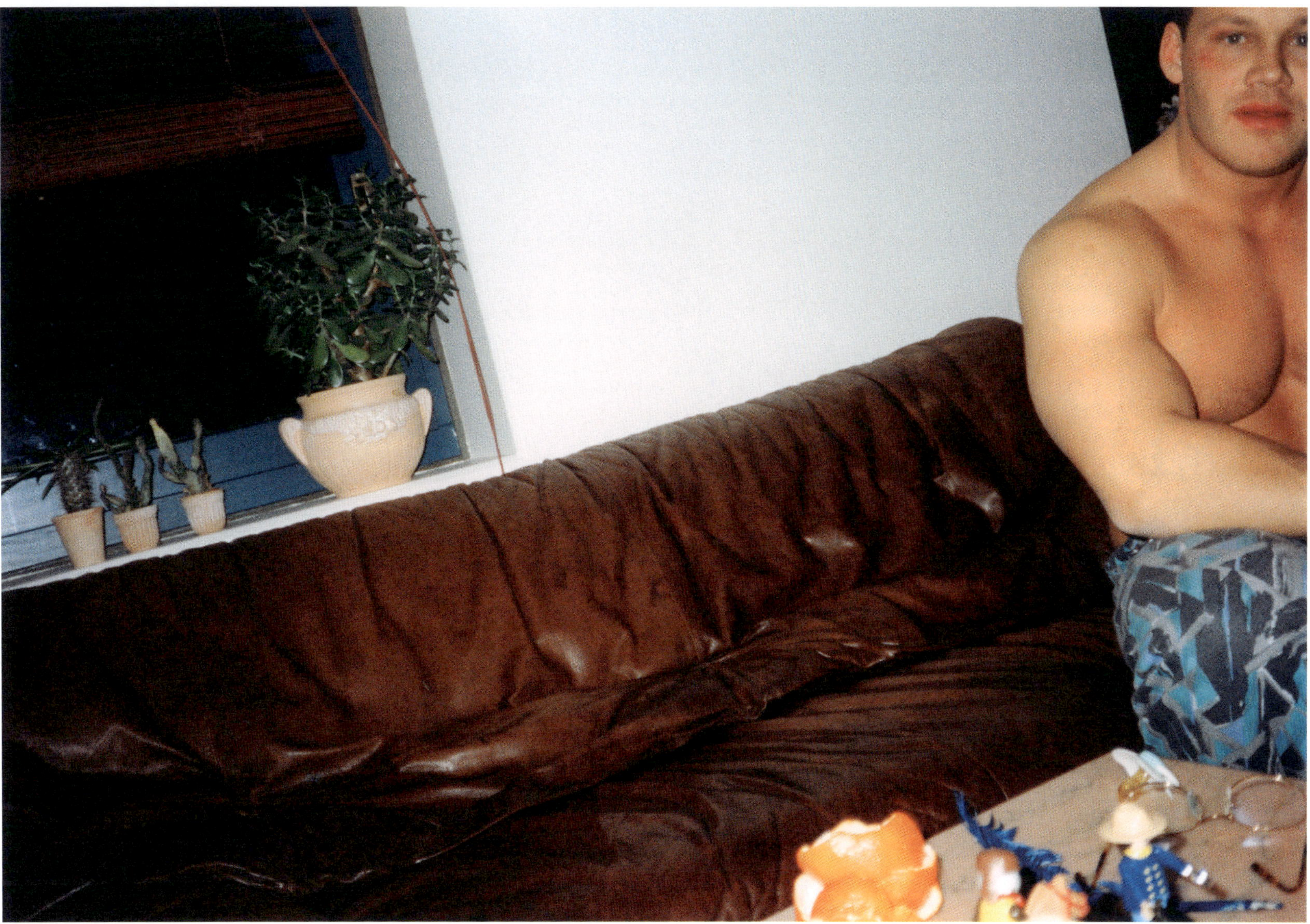

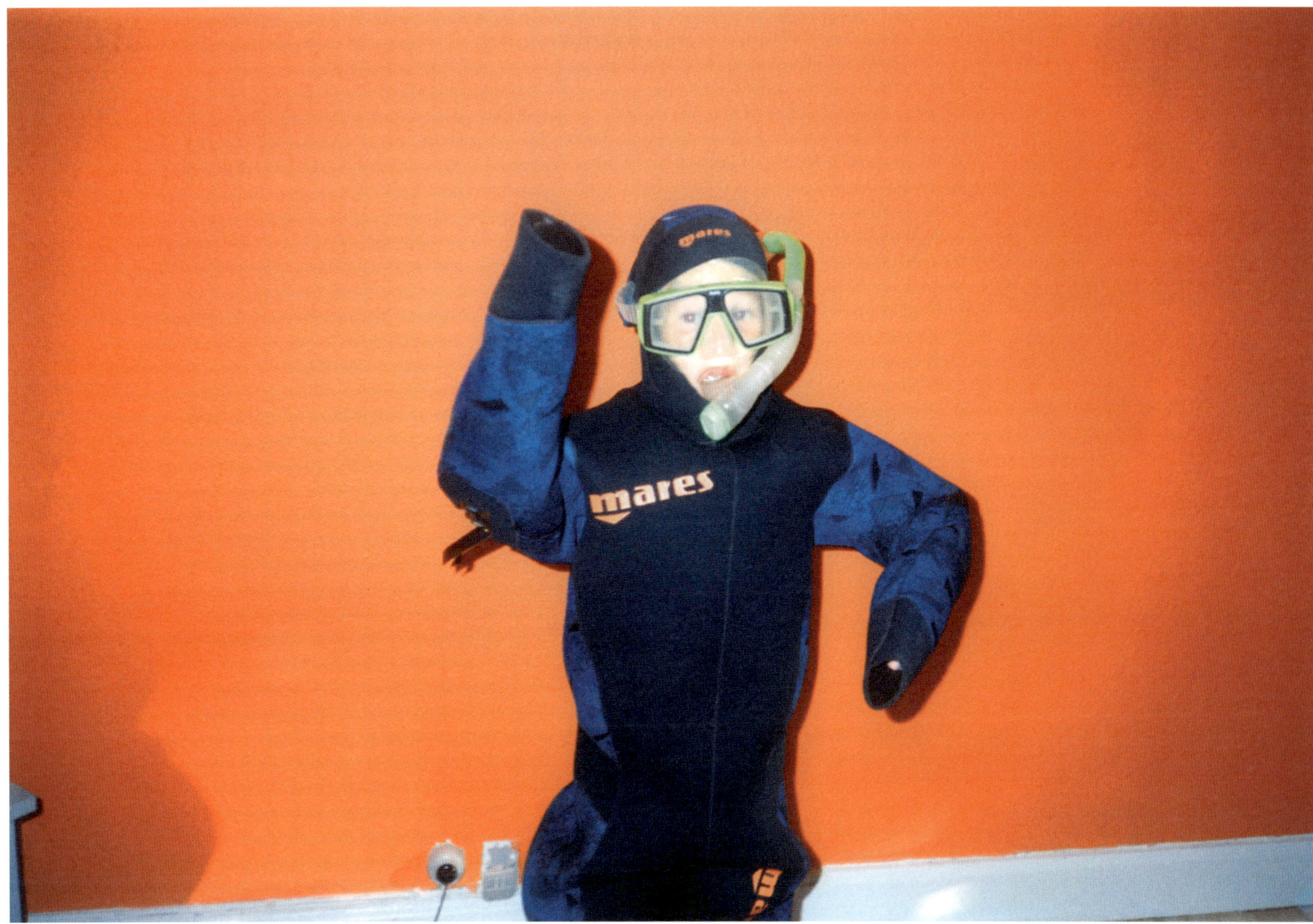
mares
mares
mares

P.S. Keep in mind "you don't get more out of it than you put into it" so when you exercise, think of me because I think of you, then the result should be good.

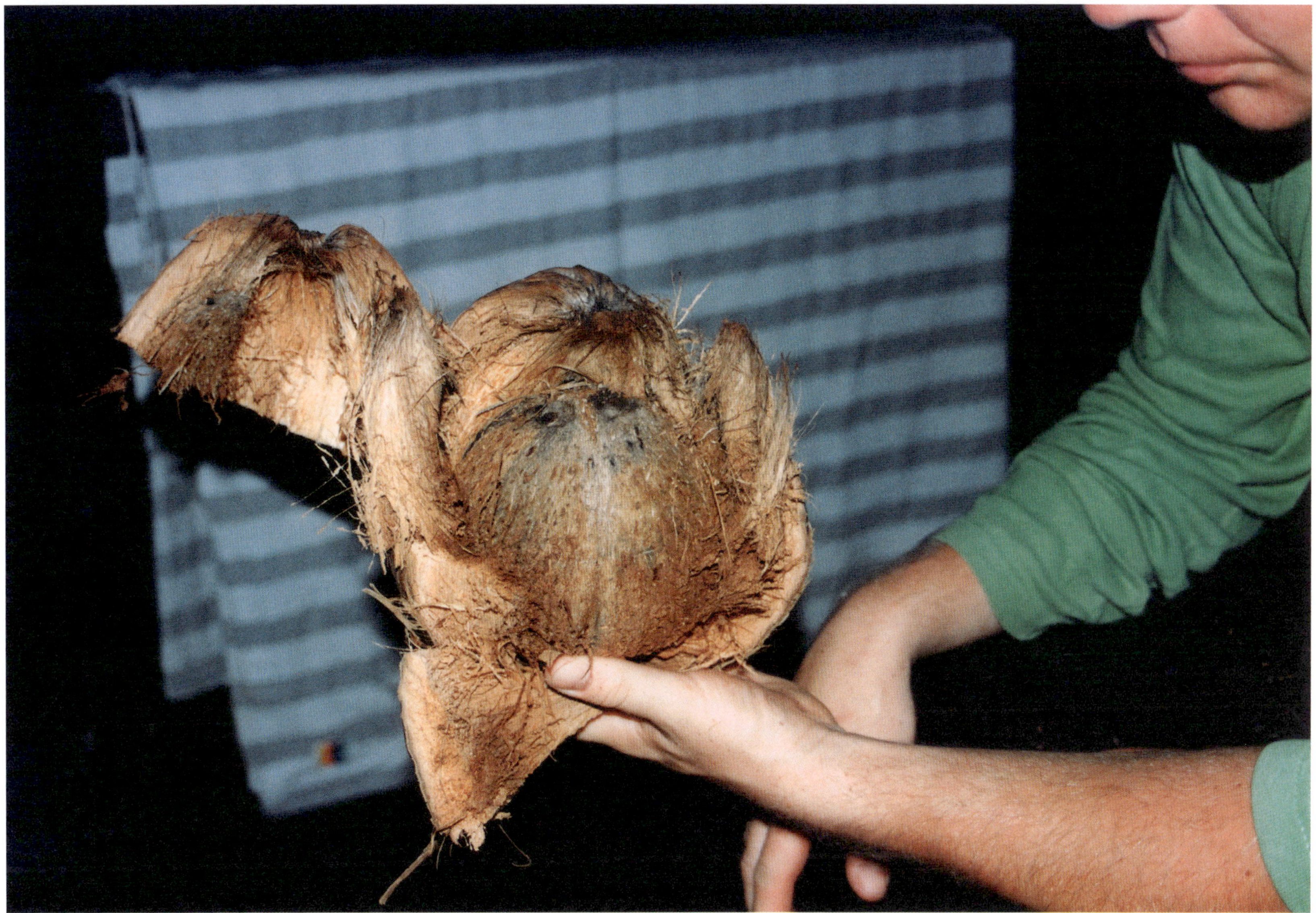

Hello "Soul Mate"
André Viking

First edition published by J&L Books
Copyright © 2025 André Viking for the images
Copyright © 2025 J&L Books for this edition

Edited by André Viking and Jason Fulford
Book design by Jason Fulford

ISBN 978-0-9993655-6-4

Printed in Denmark by Narayana Press

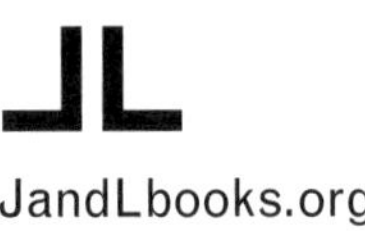

JandLbooks.org